Some Sex and a Hill

D1411663

letter to bilingualism and that curious point at which the language you speak and the person you are intersect.'
Leia Fee, Swansea, Wales

'Read the first bit, pissed myself laughing, bought it, now hooked.'
Ingi Birchell Hughes, Sir Gaerfyrddin, Cymru

'A great read - funny, inspiring, spot on about both the pleasures and challenges of
learning this beautiful and very much alive language - and solid evidence that Aran,
who has taught Welsh to thousands, really does feel our pain as learners!'
Mark Hinton, Coventry, UK

'I thought I'd just have a quick look at it before I went to bed, and over an hour and a half later I still couldn't put it down. It is laugh-out-loud funny, and an absolute page-turner.'
Lyn Goswell, Malvern, England

'This was a compulsively easy read with more than a few delighted chuckles as I recognized people, places, situations and kindred feelings about the language I too have come to love. This is the Aran Jones before SSiW as he was taking his first steps on the language journey that would change his life - and in the long run the lives of so many others. It is worth a read if

you are learning Welsh and if you are wanting to learn Welsh which is eminently possible now thanks to SSiW. Llongyfarchiadau fy ffrind i dw i'n mor falch wnes ti ffeindio y llwybr adref ac ysgythru y llwybr i ni ddilyn (I'm sure there are many errors in that sentence but hopefully the intent is clear).'
Liz Corbett, Melbourne, Australia

'This is a very entertaining account of the author's journey towards becoming a Welsh speaker in a Welsh speaking community. It is at the same time lighthearted, compassionate, and unforgiving when it comes to the importance of Welsh. I thoroughly enjoyed reading it. If you are not yet learning Welsh, start now!'
Louis van Ekert, Uralla, New South Wales

'Thoroughly enjoyable, inspiring, funny, and thought-provoking all at the same time.'
Michelle Fecio, Syracuse, New York

'The book is rather too engrossing. Reading it, I managed to overshoot my train station and had a bit of a walk to get home. This is not a good book for multitasking.'
Stuart Frankel, New York

'If you're learning Welsh, or even just thinking about learning it, read this book. The experiences of someone who has learned the language and knows

the pitfalls are incredibly valuable to a beginner. In this book, Aran Jones recounts his learning with wit and humour. It should serve as a push for anyone who has been thinking about learning the language, but hides behind such excuses as 'but I'm rubbish at languages' or 'first language speakers don't want to help me."
Karla Quadara, Melbourne, Australia

'Just started reading, and already I love this book! For anyone who has taken a Northern SaySomethingInWelsh course, you'll be able to hear Aran's lyrical voice in your head as you read. His sense of humour; warm, reassuring tone; and love for Cymru (a.k.a. Wales) shines through. Glad I bought it!'
Margaret Werdermann, Winnipeg, Canada

'This book recounts Aran Jones' decision to learn to speak Welsh, the language of his forbears, and his subsequent experiences on the way to becoming fluent. He tells of the daunting initial stages, the support of other learners, the fun that accompanies the hard work, the exhilaration of having spoken for the first time in Welsh to a total stranger and finally the joy of realising that he is actually thinking in Welsh. He speaks movingly of his love for the country, its people, language and culture. The book is written in a light-hearted style and is easily readable, but it carries a powerful message that will surely motivate others to engage or re-engage with the language of Heaven.'

John Jones, East Anglia, England

Some Sex and a Hill

or
How to Learn Welsh in 3 Easy Pints

by Aran Jones
co-founder and course
author for
SaySomethinginWelsh.com

Some Sex and a Hill or How To Learn Welsh
in 3 Easy Pints by Aran Jones

Published by:
SaySomethingin.com Ltd
94 y Ffawydd,
Llandysul, Ceredigion SA44 4JQ
www.SaySomethingin.com

© 2015 Aran Jones

For my mother, and Duncan:
who, between them, gave me a
lifelong love of language

With particular thanks to everyone
in the SaySomethinginWelsh community
who helped proofread the first edition,
and most especially Sara and Anna
for their eagle-eyed attention to detail

About the Author

Aran Jones was born in Epsom, England and brought up in Cwm Cynllwyd, y Felinheli, Guildford, Krefeld, Porches, Caravela, Tre'r Ddôl, Colombo and Kuala Lumpur.

After graduating with a less-than-entirely-useful degree in English Literature from the University College of Wales, Aberystwyth, he then worked in Aberystwyth (washing pizza dishes), Borth (staring at a swimming pool), Sarahuru (teaching English and rugby) and Dubai (more English, more rugby).

One sunny morning, he realised that he'd seen enough sand (even with added camels) and that it was time to go home, which meant he needed to learn Welsh.

After learning Welsh, he worked as an environmental consultant (much to his own surprise), an eGovernment officer (no-one knew what that meant, including his boss) and as the chief executive of a language and housing pressure group.
He then wrote an audio course for Welsh learners, and with his close friend and fellow

trouble-maker Iestyn ap Dafydd co-founded SaySomethinginWelsh.com.

Aran now lives in an overgrown garden just outside Carmel in Gwynedd, with his long-suffering wife Catrin and two children who do not know the meaning of the word 'Behave!' (in their defence, this might be partly because they don't speak all that much English yet).

You can stalk, harass or just say hello to Aran on Twitter: @aranjones

Contents

Pennod 1 – Yn y dechreuad

Oh, sure, I know exactly why you're willing to read this – it was the word 'SEX' in the title, wasn't it? Go on, admit it, you're more interested in sex than in learning Welsh – I've met your sort before, I have. Even a romp through the varied delights of 'Bod' wouldn't tempt you away from your carnal delights. Yes, I can tell. But what a waste – hours of grammar cast aside for a few breathless minutes? It's a puzzle to me. The really sad thing, though, is that sex is much better in Welsh. No, really – I'll prove it to you before the end of the book, I swear.

So we can presume you're not ready to believe me when I tell you that learning Welsh is more enjoyable than going to bed with a complete stranger? Actually, the two experiences are in many ways very similar, although there's no doubt whatsoever that having Welsh words floating around in your head the following morning is much, much more surreal than simply waking up with a stranger's elbow in your mouth. That first Welsh word, though, really is just like your first kiss; as long as your first kiss was a stressful affair with too much spit, and the worrying danger of getting caught on someone's braces thrown in for good measure. Ouch. Hey, I'm admitting nothing here.

Moving on. This little book is the story of me losing my language virginity in what was a wonderful year to be Welsh, a year of the whole damned language waking up and shouting that it wasn't going to lie there and think of England any more. 2001, and the language was very much back on the agenda, thanks mostly to the plain talking of a Gwynedd councillor by the name of Seimon Glyn. And I was there in the middle of it, shyly wanting to try out my first sentences without anyone laughing or pointing at me – edging up to people and attempting to engage them in casual, unprotected conversation.

It's also the story of the new Welsh word 'gorwir', which before August 2000 just didn't exist, which I still find hard to believe. The whole process of learning Welsh is so terminally surreal, it seems impossible that there was no way of saying 'I'm sorry, this is just too surreal for me.' 'Mae'n ddrwg gen i, ond mae hyn jyst yn rhy orwir i fi.' From 'gor', over or above, and 'gwir', the truth. Step forward and take a bow, Mr Rob Dery, a man capable of pretending to be interested in the most bizarre conversations about gorillas, as long as they're being bizarre in Welsh, and the man who stepped into the breach when we realised we could no longer continue talking to each other without a word for 'surreal'.If 'gorwir' isn't in the next edition of the Geiriadur Mawr, I may have to write a strongly worded letter. Or perhaps go on an (unusually short) hunger strike.

And the title? Well, go and look up 'some', 'sex' and 'hill' in the nearest English–Welsh dictionary, and you'll see why I try to avoid using any of them, ever, for fear of making some kind of improper suggestion. If that was all you wanted to know, you can stop reading now – although, come to think of it, there might be some sex in the next chapter.

Oh, and in the (currently unlikely!) event that you're reading this as a hard copy in Siop Y Pethe, Aberystwyth, and people are looking fluent behind the counter, and you don't feel you speak Welsh well enough to risk it, just check the price (so you know in advance what they're going to ask you for) and hand the book to them with a broad, confident smile. Smiles are the same in every language. It took me several years of being too nervous to go into Siop y Pethe at all before I worked that out, but trust me, that smile is all you need.

And one other thing – throughout this book, I will be referring to Wales as Cymru. I know it sounds a bit odd in the middle of sentences in English, and I know it might even sound like a kind of romantic attempt to pretend that I speak Welsh when really I don't. But the real reason for it, and why you're going to have to forgive me and learn to live with it, is that I don't think that we should refer to this country as Wales. It has its own name, an older, more beautiful, less mocking name (Wales just means 'the land of foreigners', after all), and that is Cymru. The land of our people. All the names we use in Cymru should be the original, real names – it doesn't matter what language someone speaks, they can learn Caerdydd for Cardiff and Casnewydd for Newport, Caergybi for Holyhead and the singing rhythm of Porthaethwy instead of the terminally literal Menai Bridge.

They can learn where they *really* live.

Some Sex and a Hill

Some Sex and a Hill

Pennod 2 – 'Mae dysgu'n gweithio'

There's something missing in your life, and you don't know what it is. You've tried ginseng, you've ordered Viagra anonymously over the internet and been disappointed, you've tried exercising more, you've tried staying in bed for longer, maybe you've even tried resigning from your job and going to live on a small Scottish island populated only by seals and people from Surrey, but there's still something missing. What are you going to do?

Well, apart from the obvious answer (call Ghostbusters, you fool), your next step has to be signing up for an Wlpan course in Aberystwyth. Oh, I know some people sing the praises of learning the language in Bangor, where there are fewer Brummies but more Scousers, some think you should go all the way down to Cardiff and be surrounded by Welsh people who think the language is only used for counting sheep, some even say you should go to

Llanbedr-Pont-Steffan where they whip you with iron wire if you even think in English, but realistically speaking it has to be Aberystwyth.

Why?

I'll tell you at the end of the chapter – for the time being, you're just going to have to take my word for it. And don't you dare go skipping pages just to find out, or the reading-books-in-the-correct-order police will have you thrown out of the country, and you'll probably end up living in London and loitering around Gray's Inn Road hoping they'll let you into the London Welsh Centre.

Aberystwyth, then. To learn Welsh, of course. Because learning Welsh fills in the gaps in your soul – 'he who cannot draw on three thousand years is living from hand to mouth', as Goethe wrote (mwy neu lai). Go on, get one of the oldest living European languages down your throat, it'll do you the world of good. Get that extra dragon tongue growing out of your mouth, the one that can sing like a stereotype and swear as colourfully as a ten-year-old Cofi.

Why did I want to, personally? That would take a serious paragraph or two.

<Serious paragraphs>

They won, you know. The administrators and government officials and mine-owners and historians and politicians who said that Welsh had to be stamped out for Cymru to be integrated more successfully into England. Here's Matthew Arnold, for example, as quoted by Saunders Lewis in 'Tynged Yr Iaith': 'It must always be the desire of a Government to render its dominions, as far as possible, homogenous... sooner or later, the difference of language between Wales and England will probably be effaced... an event which is socially and politically so desirable.' Oh, Mr Arnold, you're too kind.

But the thing is, it worked — that's why my grandparents grew up believing that Welsh was a language that would hold them back, that might even get them beaten in school; that's why my mother, taken to England when she was six, lost the language; and that's why I, except for my cradle years in Port Dinorwic and on the slopes of Aran Benllyn, grew up without it. Vulnerable, always, to the accusation that I wasn't really Welsh, silenced by the loss of a tongue that was chopped out of my mouth a generation before I was even born. So I grew up in half-a-dozen different countries, and I worked in Africa and the Middle East, and after five and half years in the desert I finally woke up one day and realised that it was time to go home.

And I'm a Cymro di-Gymraeg, a Welshman who doesn't speak Welsh, so going home means more than just a plane trip and a long wait for the bus – it means I've got a whole language to learn before I can make my peace. So yes, they won. Sort of. But thank you for that word 'probably', Mr Arnold – it makes me think of my Taid, uncomfortable in English after his stroke, and the way his clear, blue eyes would sharpen just a touch at every word in Welsh I managed. If he was still alive, I could talk to him now. They haven't sold that old lie to all of us – not yet.

</end of serious paragraphs>

So there you go – that's what saw me, in July of the year 2000, knocking on the door of the Canolfan Addysg Barhaus office in Laura Place, tucked up next to the castle, with a knot in the pit of my stomach. I was half-hoping there wouldn't be an answer, and I'd be able to escape without having to speak to a Welsh-speaking Welsh person. I didn't want to have to do that. It meant I would have to admit that I *couldn't* speak Welsh, that I had something missing, so people would stare at me. Really, that's how I felt. Learning Welsh? It's like admitting you're an alcoholic – nothing I've done since, nothing, has been even half as difficult as walking into that office, feeling ashamed, hearing Haf ap Robert say 'Bore da – ga i helpu chi?' and answering 'er… Hello.'

Hello. Look at me, I don't speak Welsh. Yup, you're not wrong, that's definitely two Ls you can hear in the middle of that Hello; I'm so bloody foreign I can't even manage Helo. Honestly, it feels like waving a Union Jack around, when everyone else has got y Ddraig Goch. No wonder I ended up wanting some kind of permanent Welsh dragon that no-one could ever take away from me – but more of that, a Dummies' Guide to making Haf scream in public, later.

And wasn't it perfect that she was dark and good-looking? Oh, wonderful, thank you God, I was hoping I'd get the chance to humiliate myself in front of an attractive woman, it's one of my favourite hobbies. I mean, here's the honest truth, people who speak Welsh are much more attractive than people who don't, and people who are stumbling pathetically in any language just don't have what it takes. Apart from the French, of course, who can hack English into a bleeding wreck and still get all the attention they want.

It's not true, though, about the Cymry Cymraeg – you know, that they'll sneer at you, and refuse to speak Welsh, and all the rest of it. There was Haf, ignoring the panic on my face, pushing forms at me, promising me there were places left on the course for August (I didn't know then that they were as likely to turn someone away as I was to start singing 'God Save the Queen'), and then asking what group I wanted to go into. Well, beginners, obviously. I've frozen, I'd get it wrong if you asked me what the Welsh for 'bore da' was, and she's talking about intermediate? Ha bloody ha.

But teachers are evil, cunning creatures. I know, I used to be one. So the next step is she's asking me questions in Welsh, simple stuff like 'Ble dych chi'n byw?', 'Beth ydy eich oedran?' and I'm answering, in English of course, because for some reason I've got some idea what she's going on about, and I'm not quick enough to realise it's a trap.

'You'll go in Intermediates, then,' she says in a smug, gotcha tone of voice, 'you understand far too much to be with the complete beginners.' I've been had, completely had, it's daylight robbery, I don't speak any bloody Welsh, that's why I'm here, for the love of God! I don't say any of this, I just think it loudly – but I can tell from the smile on her face that she can hear. Look, I want to say, it was obvious what sort of questions you were going to ask, I was working them out from the context, please please please don't put me in with people who can already speak Welsh, *please*. I was already thinking of 2B as a collection of viciously fluent, vocabulary-wielding idiom users, and not for the last time I was giving serious consideration to moving back overseas. Fortunately, I was wrong about 2B; as you'll see.

I felt like a skinned rabbit as I drove home. Nowhere left to hide anything, no more pretences. Talk about naïve – every step of the journey since then has been about learning how to fool people into thinking that I speak Welsh, but that's getting ahead of myself. Anyway, I was familiar with feeling skinned and vulnerable and bloodied, because I'd just been dumped hard-heartedly by a woman I'd wanted to marry, so panicking about learning Welsh was a useful counter-irritant.

What I didn't know at the time, what I couldn't possibly have foreseen, was how many different ways I was going to fall in love over the next few months, how many times the hole in my heart was going to be filled up with honey and balm. As I said earlier, something missing in your life? Learn Welsh. Recreate yourself. Give birth to schizophrenia – and if you don't understand that, just you wait until the first time you can't remember a word in English, because the Welsh is all you can think of. It happens, believe me.

Oh, sorry – I promised you some sex in that chapter, didn't I? I just completely forgot, I'm afraid. Don't worry, though, there'll be some in Chapter 3, almost certainly. Trust me, I'm a writer. Oh, and why it has to be Aberystwyth? The answer to that is The Cŵps.

Some Sex and a Hill

Some Sex and a Hill

Pennod 3 – Dosbarth Cyntaf

The Cŵps. Why? Because that's where I learnt at least half of all my Welsh, if not a damned sight more, stumbling down the hill at the end of the day to get some serious practice down my neck, safe in the knowledge that Brendan and Glenys weren't going to laugh at my clumsy attempts to ask for a pint. Not that 'Ga i beint, os gwelwch yn dda?' is exactly pushing the boat out, but you'd better believe I used to fret about that treiglad meddal. If it's meant to be a treiglad meddal – damn it, I'm sitting here now with a GCSE in the lingo, and I still don't have a clue. Don't tell the WJEC, though, they'll want my TGAU back. You just have to love acronyms, don't you?

Because they don't *mutate*, that's why.

I'll come back to the Cŵps later on (a phrase which sums up the entire process of learning Welsh, if you ask me) – for the time being, it's just important that you know it's there, something to keep you going

17

whenever those long afternoon lessons are making you want to scream or emigrate again or both. Keep going, the voices whisper, just a few more conjugations, it'll be time for the Cŵps soon, keep going...

Not that I knew that when I walked into my first lesson. There, you see, something else that makes it all like sex – you never, *ever* forget your first Welsh lesson. And, true to form, it's not usually because of how earth-movingly wonderful it was – nope, the scars on your memory have got a lot more to do with the panic, the awkwardness, the dread that you're going to make a right fool of yourself and that people might laugh at you. Yes, Welsh takes a lot of practice, too. And that's the understatement of the month, thrown in at no extra cost to you.

The room was hidden somewhere in the upper reaches of the Hugh Owen Building, which was my excuse for being late. We'll just forget for the time being about the four years I spent wandering around exactly those same mud-coloured corridors pretending to be learning English, okay? Yes, I did go to the University College of Wales, Aberystwyth, no, I didn't seize the chance to learn Welsh then. Because I'm pathetic, that's why, and when the second-year students told me the easiest options for Part One were Education and Philosophy, I headed straight towards the two of them as quickly as a very lazy person is capable of going. And maybe, just maybe, part of the truth is that I was too afraid to risk finding out that I wasn't properly Welsh.

So, back to the room, and to being late, because of, er… the dreadful traffic, that'll do. Yes, I'm late most of the time, and yes, I'm too old to change now. Which would have appalled the cousin of the Aunties who arrived several hours early for her tea-time visit. 'I thought I'd better not risk the train being late,' she is reported to have said (we're talking before the war here), 'so I caught the one before the one before.' It's a family thing, I guess, and it does call to something in my blood, but not quite loudly enough to get me anywhere on time.

Which leaves me walking in, bereft of language and instantly embarrassed, to a room full of people who looked so obviously fluent. Worst of all, there was David Headley, talking at them. In Welsh. Maybe that shouldn't have been such a surprise, but there you go. And they were all bloody nodding, in a 'We're fluent and we understand what he's saying' sort of way.

Bloody Haf, bloody intermediate bloody group, I thought stroppily to myself as I edged around the back of the classroom to squeeze into the only remaining chair.

'Helo,' whispered my neighbour. 'Do you go to church?' It's not true what they say about Welsh courses attracting peculiar people, it really isn't.

'No,' I wanted to whisper back. 'Do you worship the moon naked in the forest at midnight?' I didn't, though, because a) I can't think that quickly in real life, and b) I'd sworn on the fresh blood of a young goat in the night's shadow of an old stone half-way up a cold mountain that I would speak no English at all in any of the lessons. [Yes, of course you can believe me, don't be cheeky.]

Right, I thought, I'm going to sit here and smile glassily until we break for coffee, and then I'm going to go and scream at Haf. Wordlessly, just to make sure she can't scold me for speaking English. Hah. How young I was (well, comparatively), how naïve. You don't escape from a Welsh class that easily, oh no.

Actually, it all went wrong even before coffee. You see, I have a bit of an addiction – I'm a people watcher, so while I tried to time my nods to fit in with everyone else's, I was starting to spy, and imagine stories about people. Once you start making up stories about people, you have to hang around for a while to see if any of them turn out to be true. And then, just to erode my last few dregs of will-power, we started doing drills.

'O ble dych chi'n dod?'
'O ble dych chi'n dod?'
'O ble dych chi'n dod?'
'O ble dych chi'n dod?'
'O ble dych chi'n dod?'

Of course, in reality it's much less interesting than it appears on the page. No, really.

'O ble dych chi'n dod?'
'O ble dych chi'n dod?'
'O ble dych chi'n dod?'

But it does have a kind of mantra soothing effect, as your brain starts to turn to sludge, and your ability to speak begins trickling out of your ears.

'O ble dych chi'n dod?'
'O ble dych chi'n dod?'

This is all I'm going to be saying for the whole of the rest of my life, it dawns on me.

'O ble dych chi'n dod?'

And then, because I kind of understand what it means already, I make a wonderful discovery, one which will keep me in the class and nourish me in times of woe. You've probably got there before me – yes, exactly. If these people are all so brilliant at Welsh, why are we chanting 'Where do you come from?' over and over and over and over? Aha. And over and over. Unless it's some kind of monstrous plan to mock me (never discount the possibility of a plot, that's what I say), they just can't be that good after all. Well thank God. This still leaves the small matter of the intelligent-looking nodding, but the knot of sheer fear in my belly is starting to dissolve.

Coffee time that first morning, as I'm sure you can work out, was a whole barrel of laughs.

'O ble dych chi'n dod?' 'Llondon,' and a bonus mark for trying.

'O ble dych chi'n dod?' 'Canada.'

'O ble dych chi'n dod?' 'Tregaron.'

'O ble dych chi'n dod?' 'Yr Unol Da... Dal... er, America.'

'O ble dych chi'n dod?' 'America, hefyd.' Where the hell's 'hefyd', then? Oh, I see, showing off.

'O ble dych chi'n dod?' 'Llydaw.' Whoa, rewind, I'm sorry? Run that one by me again? (I'm not speaking any of these English words, you understand, I'm acting them. Yes, it's almost possible, if your face is flexible enough.) Brittany, my God. Very cool.

'O ble dych chi'n dod?' 'Lloegr.'

'O ble dych chi'n dod?' 'Aberystwyth.'

They stare at me suspiciously. Clearly, coming from Aberystwyth (if in fact I do, but that's a complicated story) is considered to be an unfair advantage. Maybe they're right – I already know where the Cŵps is. What I don't realise, as I sit there feeling temporarily smug and local, is that I am being brainwashed. Yes, brainwashed, into learning Words From The South. They're making me into a Hwntw – my Taid comes from Pen Llŷn, and they're turning me into a Hwntw! Someone call the police! I don't want this 'Ble' and 'Dod' nonsense, I need some 'Lle' and 'Dŵad' in my life – I just don't realise it at the time, to my considerable regret later on.

It's impressive how long a half-hour coffee break seems when all you can say is 'O ble dych chi'n dod?' We tailed off towards the end, of course, and just made do with smiling at each other in Welsh, trying unsuccessfully to hide the first hints of desperation in our eyes. Giles, although I didn't even really know his name at the time, was already beginning to look like a scuba diver running out of air. Then someone said, quietly, trying to pretend they were speaking Welsh, 'He does talk quickly, doesn't he?'

It was like a dam-burst. A torrent of 'Thank God somebody else thinks that too,' 'I thought I was the only one,' 'Jesus! I haven't understood a word so far,' 'D'you think he'll slow down at all?' 'I was nearly in tears at the start,' the whole gamut of nervous inadequacy bubbling up like a monstrous volcanic brew. Then a moment's silence.

'So how come all the *nodding*?' I say, and it comes out much more bitterly than I'd really meant it. I promise. They look around at each other, and then someone mutters 'Well, you know.' Fakes! The whole bloody pack of them! Faking it, pretending, *nodding* just to stop the teacher from asking any awkward questions. I could tell immediately that these were my kind of people.

And that was my last chance to escape, vanished with the morning mist, stung out of my mouth by the taste of the coffee in the refectory – I was still an innocent, then, I hadn't tried the food. I was stuck in 2B, I was going nowhere, it was time to sit back and start people-watching for real. They were a crew and a half and no mistake, a blur of colour and backgrounds and ambitions. Margaret and David, brother and sister from upstate New York tracking down their roots, Jacqueline from Llydaw who already seemed to speak far more languages than was strictly necessary, Kitty from Tregaron who'd hated school so much she'd ended up speaking more Dutch than Welsh, Marion and her cat-sanctuary ffrindiau blewog bach, Anna the post-graduate student from Cambridge who could already read mediaeval Welsh, and grumbled from time to time about how many consonants could drop out of words in a mere few hundred years. Giles from London, whom I still think of as the first person I really got to know entirely, purely through the medium of Welsh. Ansonia from Canada, Jackie from England. All sorts, a real mixture – nothing could be better for a confirmed people-watcher and part-time Welsh learner.

It may well be the best part of an intensive course – you spend so much time with the people in your group, asking question after question, playing stupid games together, suffering the same kind of pain, you get to know them so well in a month that, by the end, it feels as though you've been friends for years. And the month itself blurs – you're just left with a few scattered images from the different weeks, the moments when you laughed most or felt the most genuine desire to strangle the tutor. Welsh tutors get the blame for everything, you see – treigladau in particular. And rightly so, I say. I've heard some claim that trying to teach someone how and when 'yn' causes a soft mutation for the umpteenthfed time is *'far worse than learning the damned things in the first place'*, but quite frankly I choose not to believe that.

The highlight of that first week? Pizzas. But before I go into more detail, let's go back for a moment to this whole 'where do people come from?' thing. No, sorry, this isn't the sex bit, that's later on, probably. I just want to put it down on record how staggeringly impressive I find it when English people come here and learn Welsh. Yes, it ought to be automatic, like learning French in France, but the fact is that right now, that's not the case – which means the ones who do make the effort – well, there's something particularly valuable about them. Maen nhw'n rhoi parch i ni, dyna ydi'r peth. They place a value on us, they notice they're in a different country, they show respect. And then you hear the rabble-rousing English press churning out the same old lies about how we want to ban incomers, to kick the English out – well, to quote Paul Whitehouse, 'Arse.' Please – it's not quite your poor, your oppressed, your huddled masses, but the more people like Giles or Mike that England can send us, the better. They'll be welcomed with open arms, and they'll play their own part in keeping one of Europe's oldest and most incontrovertibly funky languages alive and kicking.

But okay, back to the pizzas. After surviving the first week, being forcefed with vocabulary and phrases until they were starting to infect our dreams (here's my standard dream at this point: someone walks up to me and starts speaking in Welsh, and I try to run away. But I figure, well, at least I'm *hearing* Welsh in my dreams), it's time for a timeout, and as far as I'm concerned that almost always means pizzas.

That was how we ended the first week, with a pizza party in the block where most of us were staying. It was a standard party, really – hanging around for a while at the start worrying that not many people were going to come, and we'd look stupid and unpopular for even trying to have a party in the first place (I told you before, never discount the possibility of a plot), then showing off by making pizza bases and keeping very quiet about the prepared mix hidden in the cupboards just in case, and then simply hoping that the alcohol would kick in and people would remember so little about it all the next day that they would just presume they had a good time. Two things about it, though, were definitely not standard party material.

The first was the fact that I was speaking no English. Yes, admittedly this meant that I wasn't exactly contributing a great deal to the party chat, but the little I did was in Welsh. I know this sounds trivial, and even maybe a little sad, but my God it was a breakthrough moment for me – I was having a party in Welsh! I was having a party, albeit a *quiet* one, through the medium of Welsh. This, I would humbly suggest, needs to be made a more central part of the process of teaching Welsh – more parties. In Welsh. Once it dawns on you that you can eat, drink and be merry without speaking English, you start to wonder what the point of English is in the first place… [If this was in an email, I'd have put a little winking smiley face after that sentence, to try and make it look as though I didn't really mean anything that sounds so offensively Anne Robinsonesque. Ho ho. As if. Etc.]

The second thing, though, was a lot more surreal. Sorry – a lot more 'gorwir'. See how often that word is needed? Well, it's an integral part of my life, anyway. The second thing was that Andrea, whom I had not previously met but who was blatantly obviously Italian, came up to me and said, in Italian, 'They say you speak Italian?'

It's always they, isn't it, the sods who sell you down the river by lying about how well you speak another language, and then sit back safe in their anonymity and enjoy watching you struggle. Clearly, I failed to deny the accusation firmly enough.

'Wonderful,' said Andrea, 'I shall speak Italian to you all the time. I have not been able to speak any Italian since I left Italy to come to Britain months ago, and I miss it.' In Italian, of course, this comes with a lot of flowery additions about beautiful languages and suchlike, but that (I *think*) was the gist of it. I, naturally, was busy thinking that's great, you do that, top idea, I meanwhile shall *avoid* you as much as is humanly possible. It was round about then I started trying to set a good example to everyone else in terms of alcohol consumption; I mean, that is the point of a party, right? And I was hoping it might work some magic in terms of my ability to remember any Italian at all.

Oh, and just in case any of you are thinking that I should have been grateful to have Italian women wanting to spend time with me, and that my willingness to *avoid* them makes it clear why it's taking so long to get any sex in this book – well, put it this way, in Italy Andrea is a bloke's name. Nice guy, but not my type.

One thing I can say, the alcohol definitely worked. Well, in terms of me waking up the next morning able to remember very little of the entire evening, let alone any particular language, and presuming therefore that I must have enjoyed myself. Which I still believe, otherwise I wouldn't want more parties on Welsh courses for everyone else – unless I was just a bitter, revengeful type of person. One other upshot was from then on, two or three times every day, I had to manage a sentence or two in Italian, with the net result that even today I still get the occasional weird urge to say something in Italian in the middle of a conversation in Welsh. Thanks, Andrea. Maybe it makes me seem cosmopolitan rather than just mad.

And to my shame, I've got to the end of another chapter without any sex. I know, I know, at least some of you were presuming that was where the party was going to end up, but look, have a heart – it's just not possible to make a fool of yourself in two languages at once and get anywhere at all in that direction. Feel free to try and prove me wrong if you'd like. In the meantime, you'll just have to wait patiently – Chapter Four, that's where it'll all kick off. Probably.

Some Sex and a Hill

Pennod 4 – Sut i Ennill Cwis Cymraeg

The start of a new week is always a weird day on an intensive Welsh course – just when you think you've started to get used to your teacher, they spring another one on you, quite deliberately, so you have to begin again, getting used to a different accent, different patterns of speech, or even just the idea that if you learn Welsh, you will have to use it to speak to more than one person. Add to that the fact that you've been away for most of the weekend, almost definitely relapsed into using English, and are starting to get disorientated by the fact that you can no longer remember anything clearly from before the start of the course, and it's quite a pit of fire for the new teacher to walk into.

Not that Rob had any problems with it – if in doubt, he falls back on poorly concealed sarcasm, a character trait which rang all sorts of immediate bells with me. We'd already been looking forward to seeing what he was like, even if only in a rather voyeuristic sort of way, because Anna had been bouncing around enthusiastically for days about the fact that he was teaching us. He'd taught her the previous year, and either she thought he was the bee's proverbials, or (and this is what I suspect) she knew in advance that he had a bit of a tendency to let people get away with speaking English.

It really can take you by surprise how quickly you learn the language on a seriously intensive course. I mean, here we were a week into it, and Ffred, Sandra and Bendigeidfran were already starting to seem like old friends. The Wlpan course, you see, is built on the ups and downs of Ffred, a Welsh learner, Sandra, the first-language Welsh speaker who's prepared to run away from her non-Welsh-speaking husband to be with Ffred (so I'm far from the first person to realise how closely sex and learning Welsh are related), and their dog Bendigeidfran, who is by quite some distance the most intelligent of the three. It's touched by genius – the thoroughly unreliable Ffred puts himself up for elections and is lucky even to get Bendigeidfran's vote, irritates Sandra by fancying his Welsh tutor, gets into a punch-up with Sandra's ex-husband when the ex tries to run over Bendigeidfran, and considers end-of-course Welsh parties as clearly more important than the birth of his and Sandra's first child. A perfect role model for any would-be Welsh learner, and a million miles from the ordinary boring families that language learning courses tend to be built around. It's worth learning Welsh just to meet the three of them, and real Welsh speakers are, generally speaking, even more entertaining.

Outside the two Ffred and Sandra excerpts a day, most of what we were doing was, apart from the drills, stories. Written, spoken, in pairs, in groups, it was all essentially telling stories, and this was where Giles began to come to the fore.

He'd started the week despairingly, claiming at coffee time on the first morning that he was actually forgetting Welsh faster than he was learning it, and that by logical progression he would soon be able to speak no languages at all; but once we got into the story-telling, he really brightened up, and to this day I believe he would be a better pulp journalist than geography lecturer. Except for one minor drawback – it became evident very early on that he was incapable of adding a single paragraph to any of our collective stories without including something about a gorilla. No clear reason springs to my mind immediately as to why a geography lecturer should suffer from this kind of obsession – if he was a zoologist it might make sense, but geography? And perhaps even more worrying than Giles's own personal interior landscape was the speed with which the gorilla became the class mascot – no-one else could write anything without bringing the bloody gorilla into it too. Stories would build up paragraph by paragraph around the class, and you'd just know that a huge hairy beast was going to spring into them from somewhere. 'It was a dark and stormy night, and their car broke down. They climbed out into the rain, and began to walk towards an old house. It was empty, and there was no-one around. Then they saw the gorilla.' Yes, worrying stuff.

Of course, it did have one good knock-on effect – if my memory serves me correctly, it was after a gorilla escapade of some kind that we cornered Rob into inventing the word 'gorwir' for us. Necessity is the mother of invention and all that. From then on, it was like a classroom complaint – 'Please, sir, Giles is being gorwir again.' Into his stride by now, though, Giles was not to be denied, and before we knew where we were, the next thing he forced upon us was the word 'corgimwch'. I can honestly say that in over ten years since first learning the word, I have not had to refer to shrimps in normal conversation a single time. Inevitably, Giles claimed that it was quite ordinary to know words like 'corgimwch', but people who spend a lot of their time going scuba-diving clearly have slightly different views of life than the rest of us. Mind you, as a baptism by fire, it certainly works – if you can wait patiently in the queue (one of those rare words which is easier to spell in Welsh than in English) for food in the Arts Centre (or, as we were increasingly ambitiously attempting to refer to it, Canolfan y Celfyddydau) with someone talking about shrimps in a loud voice, you're certainly not going to be embarrassed later on by trying to talk to Cymry Cymraeg. And even if you are, hey, just throw a few shrimps into the conversation. That shuts anyone up.

There's something infectious about people in Welsh classes. Yes, I know that sounds quite unpleasant, but I don't mean it like that. You just can't help picking things up from them, you see. Obviously, I will never be able to forget the word 'corgimwch', no matter how hard I try, and by early in the second week, I was already starting to lose my ability to resist Kitty's hypnotically regular use of the word 'lot'. Ah, yes, you look at that and you think it's an English word, don't you? How pitifully wrong. The sheer fact of the matter is, you already speak some Welsh, and you just didn't realise it. The Welsh word 'lot', just so you don't get confused here, means 'many or a large number'. Kind of accessible, isn't it? And for Kitty, it was obviously something of a security blanket – any time she was under pressure, out would come 'lot' – 'wel, er, lot, wel, mae 'na lot...' The thing was, though, it made her sound rather fluent, which was completely unfair. She had a good accent, which helped, but there was just something so appealing about the casual ease with which she'd go lotting away – and the upshot is that 'lot' is now probably one of the words I use most often. Yes, I know 'llawer' is a perfectly good word, but I'm sorry – saying 'lot' reminds me of Kitty bouncing around and being cheerful or intense or cheerfully intense all at the same time. It's too late for me to change now. A lot too late.

One of the best bits of an intensive course is the effort made by the organisers to arrange out-of-class entertainment – through the medium of Welsh, naturally. A perfect opportunity, if you've only just started learning, to feel completely lost, overwhelmed by a tidal wave of incomprehensible sounds, but not to worry too much about it, because you're surrounded by friendly attitudes and plenty of medicinal alcohol. As I sit here writing this, my first Welsh quiz night (in the Cŵps – now there's a surprise) comes back to me uncannily vividly. Now, I'd like to start by making it perfectly clear that I do not believe in that ridiculous suggestion that taking part is more important than winning. I'm not even sure if breathing is more important than winning. I play to win, and if I have to use an axe to do so, well, I'm sorry, that's just the way it is. In fact, to digress momentarily, it would be wonderful to see our national rugby team approach their matches with the same kind of almost-psychotic need for victory as I take to pub games. I can just see an English centre breaking through in midfield, thinking he's got a clear run for the line, and then being felled by a viciously hurled tomahawk from the full-back. Or one of those ninja throwing star things, maybe. All sorts of entertaining possibilities.

Anyway, the first clue to success in a Welsh quiz night is, obviously, get a Welsh speaker on your team. Simple but effective. In fact, that's pretty much the only clue to success in a Welsh quiz night – apart from the standard quiz stuff: shouting out the wrong answer, throwing beer at people who look as though they'll get the answer if they can just think clearly for a moment, looking over the quiz-master's shoulders on your way back from an unnecessary trip to the little boys' room, all the old traditional options. We had been cunning enough to bribe Rob with alcohol (not too much, you've got to keep them effective, a Welsh speaker in a drunken coma is less help than you would think), and felt confident from the start. Actually, I was lying when I said it comes back to me vividly – it comes back to me in a sort of blurred, beer goggles kind of way, with the single exception of our quite phenomenally outstanding charades. Before you mock, have a go yourself at acting out 'An Englishman Who Went Up a Hill and Came Down a Mountain' with a group of seven alcoholics. The bit where we tried to lift up the chair with some poor fool standing on it was comic genius, and nobody actually had to go to hospital afterwards, so you can't accuse us of carelessly risking life and limb. Unless you're one of those tedious people who think you can say something just because it's true.

And then there was something else we had to do, carried away with the thrill of success, and I can't for the life of me remember what it was – only that it was based around a staggeringly clever bilingual pun involving 'Haf' sounding like 'Half', and leading to us all lying down to act out sunbathing. The lying down bit was a relief, I can tell you that much.

Well, it seemed witty at the time.

And this last bit I don't like admitting, because it shows worrying signs that I might be starting to get old. But out with it – the grizzly truth is that I can't actually remember who won the damned thing. I know, I know, what kind of semi-psychotic victory-obsessed lunatic am I? Clearly not up to scratch. My suspicion is that we must have lost – I'm sure I would have remembered if we'd won, because it would have involved wild celebration and finding people to be smug at.

Then you wake up the next morning, and you've got all the standard problems to deal with (breath that hurts your lips, somebody else's dead tongue in your mouth, bowels that... well, let's skip that bit), and then suddenly something dawns on you. Yes. It's true. You spent the evening speaking Welsh.

The first time that hits you, it's a hell of a feeling. It doesn't matter how Neanderthal your conversation may have been, it doesn't matter that the charades were just an extension of how you were having to communicate anyway, it doesn't matter that the floor of the room upstairs in the Cŵps is littered with the mangled, bloody results of your attempts to use mutations, it doesn't matter that you couldn't currently construct a sentence in any language under the sun to save your life.

You spent the evening speaking Welsh.

I'm not even going to bother trying to describe the mood that leaves you in. Mostly because I know perfectly well I'm not a good enough writer, and I never try to do anything I think is too difficult for me. 'If at first you don't succeed,' my motto is, 'see if you can pretend you weren't really trying.' But believe me, it is a feeling that is worth every moment of despair, humiliation or embarrassment, worth every single mutilated mutation, worth whatever it took you to get there. Yes, even worth walking into an Wlpan office where you know they're going to speak Welsh and saying 'Hello' in English.

***

One of the drawbacks that starts to become apparent as you approach the mid-point of the course is how many times you have had the same conversation. Sometimes with different people, sometimes with the same person over and over again. They like to make you change seats on a regular basis, so you don't just talk to the same person for the whole month, but usually this just means that everyone gets up, swaps over to the other side of the classroom, and sits down next to the same person again. Even if you're a good person at heart, and do what you're told, you still end up having a lot of déjà vu conversations. Or déjà entendu, as a tiresomely clever friend of mine once put it. But fair play to Aberystwyth, it rather saves the day by offering plenty of variety in your conversations about the weather. You can usually get a whole paragraph just by looking out of the window: 'Mae hi'n braf heddiw. Wps. Mae hi'n niwlog heddiw. Wps eto. Mae hi'n bwrw glaw eto. Diwrnod hyfryd arall yn Aberystwyth.'

Oh, in passing, another top tip for why to choose Aberystwyth as the location for your course – 'A' doesn't mutate. Bangor, Cardiff? Look out, duck, incoming mutilations. As for Llandbedr-Pont-Steffan, well that's just downright bloody hard to say. And it mutates. Probably.

So, anyway, you get pretty bad RCI after a while – Repetitive Conversation Injury. A bit like when you type too much, but a lot (trademark Kitty) more painful. I can remember the first time it hit home too hard to be ignored; I was sitting at a table in the Canolfan with Giles, eating something that, fair play to them, tasted as good as you'd expect for that kind of price, and he just snapped. One corgimwch too many, I suspected at the time.

'I'm sorry, I know we're not meant to speak English, but I've just had enough. My brain is melting. If I don't have a real conversation soon, I'm going to kill someone. I don't want to talk about the weather, I don't want to talk about learning Welsh, I don't want to talk about where I come from. Can we just take a half-hour timeout and talk about politics or art or bloody anything proper? *Please?*' If you're wise, you do not even consider arguing with someone who sounds that desperate. Especially not if you're feeling more or less the same thing. And yes, it was an enormous relief; like that slice of chocolate cake in the middle of your diet. You know it's not helping, but you're really past caring, just for the moment.

But pat on the back for us, we didn't give in to the binge instinct; it really was just that half hour, and then it was time to gather our books, stand up, look out of the wide, tall windows, and say, in a resigned, gird-your-loins tone of voice,

'Mae hi'n bwrw glaw heddiw. Eto.'

I suppose it's no surprise that your brain starts functioning and misfunctioning so oddly when you really go at it flat out learning another language. I've read somewhere (always quote your sources, unless you're just too careless to be able to remember them in the first place) that mental activity – like, for example, playing chess or training your memory – actually changes the way your brain works. Neurons fire regularly enough to create something equivalent to a reflex, or some such scientific mumbo-jumbo. Almost, really, physically changes the shape of your brain. Now, while I wouldn't suggest for a moment that you believe me (not least on the grounds that I very rarely believe myself), it does make you think, doesn't it? All sorts of unexpected aspects of who you really are start to change when you begin to grow the skin of a second language. You learn new ways of thinking about things, you discover new attitudes, you become more than you were before. And you meet women.

What more could you want?

Oh, the gory details about the whole meeting women thing? Well, I've run out of space here, so we'll just have to leave that until the end of the next chapter. Hope you don't mind.

Some Sex and a Hill

Pennod 5 – Tatws a Threigladau

Wait a minute, hang on, is that Rob's week gone already? That's the problem with trying to be sensible and do this chapter by chapter. I've not had time to talk about our end of the week goodbye dinner in the Indian restaurant at the end of the Pier. I haven't had time to complain about Rob's tendency to start sudden and interesting conversations in English, which makes it very hard to remain pure and Welsh (yes, the two do go together). I haven't even had time to thank him for sensitising us to the sound shift between 'hwyl' and 'hoyw' – one means goodbye, the other means gay, and getting them the wrong way round confuses everyone. One of my fellow learners shouted 'Gay, Rob!' instead of 'Goodbye, Rob!' at the end of one session, and we gained a new respect for the tricky waters of farewell. 'Hwywy… ta-ra!' we would go, uncertainly, as we left lessons from then on.

Oh, and just before moving on, I would like to make one thing completely clear. Rob is not shy or silly, as other books in which he has appeared make him sound; he does not blush easily (if at all), he is not childishly enthusiastic in class, and no-one could accuse him of being fey. He is, by contrast, rough, tough and hard to bluff, a Charlton Heston of the Welsh-tutoring world, a man you wouldn't want against you in a bar brawl.

Is that better, Rob?

Now, it's time for a brief escape from the pattern of class after class and teacher after teacher. Why? Because, over the weekend, we went to the National Eisteddfod. Oh, okay, I'll own up, I can't for the life of me remember if that really was the weekend we went to the National Eisteddfod, but we definitely went at some point during the course, and talking about it in the middle of the month is, well, neat and tidy.

The Eisteddfod. I doubt that there is a better time or place to consider the differences between those of us lucky enough to be brought up speaking Welsh, and those of us brought kicking and screaming to the language at a later age. The trip down to the Eisteddfod, in Llanelli, was, to be honest, entirely nerve-wracking. The closer we got, the more I succumbed to a sense of panic at the prospect of being in wide open spaces surrounded by Welsh speakers. I was excited, too, of course – I know it may sound a little quaint, but it was my very first Eisteddfod of any kind, local or national, and it was something I would never, never have had the courage to do before starting to learn Welsh. It felt like a staging-post, an achievement of some kind – I was prepared to spend the day vulnerable to the possibility that people might speak Welsh at me without giving me any chance at all to prepare my answers beforehand.

I did have sensible defensive measures in mind, of course. I was going to hide in a corner of the Pabell y Dysgwyr (the Learners' Tent), and if I had to go out at all I was going to stay very close to Giles (who was quite prepared to talk about shrimps with anyone) and pretend that I was *deaf*.

Now, compare that to the sense of world-weary, been-there done-that tiredness that seems to come over some first-language Welsh speakers at the prospect of the National Eisteddfod, and it's clear that there will be an attitude gap there for ever. For me, any Eisteddfod will always be an oddly magical thing, because it will always remind me that I'm speaking Welsh – no-one ever had the chance to force me to go to them when I was a child, and to sing or dance when I didn't want to, so I never developed that stubborn resistance.

Besides, I wasn't worried at all, oh no. I was virtually fluent. I could even say 'Eisteddfod'.

Four things stay in my mind from that day out in Llanelli. To begin with, there was the sheer awkwardness with which I psyched myself up to ask for food from the hot potato stall. I knew what I wanted, I'd limited my choices and checked my vocabulary, but I still didn't much like the thought of talking to someone who might answer with a sentence that wasn't written in a book. It was absolutely infuriating, really, honestly *maddening*, when I finally (driven by a very real and increasing need for food) asked for a baked potato with cheese (I didn't really want cheese, but I wasn't sure if there was a Welsh word for tuna), and was answered with 'Wot? You wanna potato?'

'I'm sorry?' I thought. 'This is the Eisteddfod, am I right? You are speaking *English* to me after I have made the bloody effort to learn some Welsh?' I know, I should have said it, not just thought it, but I was so focused on speaking in Welsh, it wasn't easy to let go, certainly not quickly enough to be stroppy. Talk about a let down. Thousands of miles all the way down to Llanelli to attend my first ever Eisteddfod, an hour and a half preparing a neat little request for food that didn't involve any mutations, and some swine was speaking *English* at me? I almost lost my appetite.

(Almost.) Is it really too extremist (and aggressive and racist and all that rubbish) to expect that people working in the National Bloody Eisteddfod learn enough Welsh to take orders in the language the whole damned thing is meant to be *celebrating*? In fact, remembering it now makes me feel quite irritated all over again, and I'm a placid enough person usually. If, by some fluke of chance, you *are* the person who was serving baked potatoes in English on the Saturday of the Llanelli Eisteddfod, the first Eisteddfod of the new millennium... well, I've built an online Welsh course for you. It's called SaySomethinginWelsh.com. You can have it for free. Oh, hell, I'll PAY you to take it. *Call* me.

I've forgotten the other three things now, I'm feeling so retrospectively irritated. No, hang on, they're coming back. The second may sound even more stupid than usual, but hey, I was brought up (in Portugal rather than Cymru, but you can't have everything, and at least we could go swimming in the sea at Christmas) on 1970s Welsh rugby. We would crouch next to the radio listening to Cymru win over and over again, so of course I was unreasonably thrilled to hear Ray Gravell giving some kind of prize award type talk in the little amphitheatre kind of place. And I could even Understand Some Of What He Was Saying – these are the moments which make a learner feel that something powerful and new is happening to them, and they're moments which it's very hard to share with anyone who has never lost the language and had to struggle to win even some of it back.

The third moment? Ah, that would be realising that the several large bags of sweets, the various helpings of junk food, and the fudge had not really been the best way to prepare for the large portion of ice-cream with strawberries on top. It rather took my mind off the Eisteddfod, the feeling that I was quite possibly going to throw up extensively and impressively in front of a great number of people. I thought briefly (and incorrectly) that I would rather have been guilty of a public mismutation. The whole too-much-food thing cast something of a shadow over the last hour or so, I'm sorry to say. But look, it's an important cultural part of the Eisteddfod, I think – if there are lots and lots of different little stands selling different kinds of food, it's a kind of cultural and economic responsibility for you to try and support as many of them as possible. Isn't it?

Which leaves me feeling a little guilty about the fourth and last thing that I remember. I'm sorry to say that after I was quite sure that the ice-cream wasn't going to make me throw up after all, I, er. Well. I sort of thought it might be quite a long journey home, so I thought it would be sensible to have one last baked potato before I left. I'm fully aware that this makes me sound like a particularly greedy imbecile, but... well, there we are.

That's not what's memorable about it, though. What is memorable, in a cringingly embarrassing sort of way, is that after a whole day of concentrating, trying not to make a fool out of myself, understanding little bits of Welsh and speaking the odd word or two myself, I was entirely unprepared for the potatoes. I knew from experience that they spoke English, you see, and I was tired, and if you send me a stamped addressed envelope I'll send you another five hundred equally weak excuses. But shame, shame on me, I ordered my potato in English. There, I've admitted it. I hang my head.

Not quite as much as I hung my head, however, when they answered in Welsh.

Oh, embarrassment, how I love your tender charms.

The only thing I have to offer in my defence is that I was, by this stage, loaded down with almost my own body weight in pointless tacky tourist gift items, which is the other main purpose of the Eisteddfod, as far as I can see. So at least I was contributing to the local economy.

And I've got away without admitting that I fell asleep in the main pavilion while listening to a male voice choir.

Oops, damn it, did I say that out loud? I deny it, no such thing ever happened. I'm Welsh, for heaven's sake, I could never find a male voice choir boring, I know how to live up to my national stereotypes.

So that was my first Eisteddfod. It won't be my last, though. I plan on forcing myself to attend every year for the next twenty, even if I find myself living outside Cymru again, just to try and see if I can recreate that first-language Welsh-speaking sense of reluctance. Nobody can say I'm not aiming for the full package. Alternatively, I might just take the easier route and have children at some point, and then gleefully force them to go to every single eisteddfod within a hundred-mile radius, just to make sure they get that genuine 'mention the Urdd and I'll scream' Welsh upbringing. The sins of the fathers are meant to be visited upon the little children, aren't they?

Unfortunately, the contented glow of having survived the Eisteddfod without throwing up even once didn't last long, because back in Aberystwyth at the start of the next week I was treated to the single most negative experience I've had while I've been learning Welsh.

It did a lot to make me realise that the language needs to be defended actively — that some people are so bitter and hostile towards it, so lacking any understanding of its beauty and value, that left to themselves they quite honestly would just want to see it dead. It's a sickening thought that people can be so mindlessly vicious, but we have to be aware of it — because there is no middle ground in the face of that kind of enmity. Either we win, or they do.

What made it worse was that I thought he was a friend. I'd known him, after all, since I was a guitar-mad student at Aberystwyth, and that had been more than a decade before. I knew his wife, I knew his kids (both of whom were going through a bilingual school system and spoke good Welsh), I thought I knew him. I'd been keen, when I saw him on campus, to meet up for lunch — I thought he'd be interested in what I was doing. He'd claimed, after all, that he'd tried to learn Welsh when he first moved here — but I should, perhaps, have seen the warning signs in the way he blamed Welsh people for not having been nice enough to him while he was learning. It was their fault, of course, that he hadn't carried on.

The attack, when it came, took me completely by surprise. I was expecting to be asked why I was learning Welsh — people tend to be genuinely interested. What I wasn't expecting, once I'd given my standard quick blurb about wanting my language back, was his next comment.

'But what's the point? It's dead anyway, no-one speaks it any more.'
For a moment I thought he must be joking, but then his wife joined in, repeating what he'd said, and he carried on.

'I get it all the time at the University, students writing their essays in Welsh, and then we have to hang around and wait for a translation. They're so selfish. They all speak English, anyway. It's pathetic.'

I felt dizzy. This was meant to be my friend, and he was telling me that my language and culture had no right to survive, because his language and culture were bigger and better.

'There's only about fifteen percent speak it any more, it's just a complete waste of time.' You see the kind of self-deluding nonsense that people like that subscribe to? He was living in Ceredigion, where the last census figures available at that point showed that more than 60% spoke Welsh. It was the majority language around him, and he had persuaded himself that it didn't really exist. Willing, deliberate, malicious blindness. And he chose to live here – the option of going back to England was always available to him, if he really found our language so offensive. But of course there was no need for that – he was just hanging on and looking forward to the day it died out. How many more people like that are living in our midst, with the right to vote on the future of a country that they wish didn't exist?

I can't really remember how I got away from them, after choking down what was left of my sandwich. All that remains is the sense of overwhelming relief at being back with my friends on the course – not only because they spoke Welsh, but because they were civilised, liberal human beings who respected other people, other cultures and other languages. I knew that I had lost a friend, because there was no way in which I could tolerate his viciousness towards something I loved. I also knew, though, that I had lost a friend who had not been worth having in the first place – a pity that it had taken me ten years to find out what he really thought about my people.

I've seen him once since then, walking past each other on the campus. He said 'Hello' and I said 'Bore da', without even noticing that I was speaking Welsh. Despite everything, it's a friendship I'd like back – but only if he managed to find the respect to speak to me in my language.

And I have a feeling that won't happen.

Some Sex and a Hill

Pennod 6 – Brad y Cardiau Gleision

Week Three was Heulwen week. That's right, you're settled, you're almost understanding some of Rob's really weird ways of pronouncing perfectly respectable words (odd-oo? I'm sorry?), and then they go pulling you out of the comfort zone and reminding you that there are still, against all the odds, more than two different people who speak Welsh.

Heulwen week was particularly memorable for two distinct reasons, as far as I was concerned. Mostly, for the treachery of the blue cards, the very memory of which makes my brain ache again, but also for the slow (you could even say belated, and look at me pitifully) realisation that there are people who live almost their entire life through the medium of Welsh. Really, honestly, people who have very little occasion to speak English, and who are much more comfortable when they don't.

I don't know why I didn't realise this before, because Heulwen wasn't our first tutor — but for some reason, maybe the way she spoke about her home, her family life, it was made unavoidably clear that she really found it a little odd that people spoke English.

Let me put this into context — I'm typing this in Gwynedd, I know perfectly well by now that a life largely free from English is entirely possible, but at the time I was new back to Cymru, new back to the language, and I was suffering from one of the most common diseases amongst non-Welsh speakers. I didn't really believe, or I didn't really understand, that it was a living, breathing language.

I feel a little ashamed to admit that now — but if you live your entire life through the medium of English, and if you don't speak Welsh, then everyone speaks English around you. If you're lazy you can let yourself believe that you're just not meeting Welsh speakers. But the truth is, throughout much of Cymru, huge great swathes of territory in the north and the west, there are still more people who speak Welsh than do not.

That's an important point. Welsh is NOT a minority language, not in a hell of a lot of places it's not. It's about time people realised this, and made the effort to learn it before moving into Welsh-speaking areas.

Back to Heulwen – as I realised that she was less comfortable in English than in Welsh, a feeling of, I don't know, something a bit like joy hit me. It's hard to explain, and probably needs a better writer – but the understanding that this language that was slowly making itself at home in my mouth and my mind was in fact alive, kicking, and quite capable of providing all the words you could ever need for your entire life... it was beautiful.

Although, I suspect, perhaps not quite as beautiful for the stubborn few in the class who were ready to slip back into English as and when they could. Heulwen was far less tolerant of English in the classroom than either Rob or even David had been, and I found myself hoping enthusiastically that we were going to see some kind of 'English Not' enforced for the rest of the week. But no. Instead, we were going to see something far, far worse.

The blue cards.

Simple, but effective. I've never seen mental torture of that kind before, and I hope very much that I never see it again, except in films about prisoner of war camps and heroically resistant English chaps, where it belongs. In fact, come to think of it, maybe Heulwen was originally inspired by 'A Bridge over the River Kwai'.

Okay, okay, I'll explain it, and you'll laugh at me because it will sound so harmless, but you try it. Just you try it yourself, and see how much you laugh then.

Blue cards. A pack of them, say about the same as in a pack of normal cards. (It took me a long time to recover enough to be able to play cards again, but that's another story.) Simple so far, right? Now, on one side of the cards is a word in Welsh, and on the other is the translation into English. At this point, you can see that the course is starting to work on me – I'm already beginning to consider all words as existing originally in Welsh, and only becoming English when someone translates them. Anyway, the cards. I know, it really doesn't sound that bad. Well, here's the key bit.

They're all different tenses.

I'm sorry, you don't appear to be shaking in your seat with mortal fear yet. Let me repeat that, a little more loudly. They're all different tenses!

You just don't get it, do you? Okay, here, hold my hand. You start off, for example, with 'I am walking' – 'Rydw i'n cerdded.' Great, yes, simple, easy. Then you get 'I will be walking' – 'Bydda i'n cerdded.' Still no problem? Of course not. Then 'I walked' – 'Wnes i gerdded.' How unpleasant, a mutation, but worse things happen at sea. Then it's 'I was walking' – 'Ro'n i'n cerdded.' 'I had walked' – 'Ro'n i wedi cerdded.'

Starting to sweat yet? 'I will have walked' – 'Bydda i wedi cerdded.' How are your pain tolerance levels? 'I would walk' – 'Byddwn i'n cerdded.' 'I would have walked' – 'Byddwn i fod wedi cerdded.' Why the hell is there a spare 'bod' in there? Good God, don't ask me.

You're obviously not in enough pain, and meanwhile I can't possibly carry on any longer. The difference is, you're just reading these, in a row – to get the agony going, you need to be shown one side of a card, and be expected to say whatever is on the other side. No, I agree, on its own that is entirely survivable. Then it happens again. Then again. And again and again and again and again and bits of your brain start melting I absolutely guarantee you and again and again and again. Please, please feel free to try, and see how long you can go before you get tears in your eyes. And again and again and again and agarghghghghgliddly…

Before we started the blue cards, I was quite confident that I knew my tenses (well, apart from the future, fair cop guv'nor). I have never since been able to remember what you say when for which tense when ever since. See, did that sentence make sense? I just don't know any more.

And while you're suffering this, Heulwen is laughing at you. Oh, okay, not actually laughing, but you can tell that she finds it quite funny when you start to beg for mercy, and there are tears in your eyes. That's how she reacted to my despair, anyway. Perhaps, of course, she just suspected I was a Gog at heart, and was enacting some kind of pre-emptive strike. If so, it worked, and it's why I mumble so much of the time even now.

I was still mute and trembling when we walked down the hill that evening to listen to Siân James play harp upstairs in the Cŵps. I had a feeling that I'd seen her play before, at the Phoenix festival near Reading in 1996, but thanks to the after-effects of the blue cards, there was no way I could work up the Welsh or the courage to ask her if I was right. Siân James is a cultural treasure that the di-Gymraeg are largely robbed of – she sings in Welsh, so the English-language media seem to decide to themselves 'nobody'll be able to understand her, so let's not bother letting them know she exists'. She's got one of the most distinctive and intoxicatingly beautiful voices you'll hear anywhere in the world, strong enough to seem almost operatic when she wants, and endlessly creative – I've never heard blues played on the harp before – and I felt as though the pleasure of listening to her was a just and fitting reward for the efforts I was putting into trying to come home. Learning Welsh will open up so much more for you than there is any way of realising until you start actually doing it – films, books, singers, comedians, there is an entire and endlessly fascinating culture that, if you don't speak Welsh, is always just out of sight round the corner, heard faintly in the distance. All you have to do is learn the words, and suddenly it's at full volume. If you're not sure that you believe me, buy Sian James's album 'Pur' – that'll make the point far more powerfully and convincingly than I ever could.

Heulwen week was also memorable for David and Margaret's deeply, deeply peculiar noise-sensitive landlord and landlady. David and Margaret had rented a flat in the town, you see – they were both university professors, so they knew perfectly well that student accommodation is designed for people who have yet to become fully human, and they had no intention whatsoever of making the mistake of booking into a hall of residence.

What they weren't, though, was the kind of university professors you would *necessarily* want teaching your children. I can't remember now whether it was David or Giles who started the whole idea of 'revision sessions' every night in the Cŵps, but it became a completely obviously natural habitat for both David and Margaret. It still shocks me slightly when I walk into the Cŵps now and they're not already sitting in one of the corners with a couple of pints of Guinness in front of them. Margaret, in particular – 'No, no, I'll not have another, I'm just about to go back to the flat, I've got a lot of revision to do on "Bod" tonight and I've promised myself okay but just the one.'

David, by contrast, would never even start the 'Maybe I should go home now' sentence – in fact, he was much more likely to be the one ordering you another pint despite the fact that you are hunched language-less in the corner begging mutely to be allowed to go home because it is way way past midnight and you can no longer feel your tongue. Happy memories.

Anyway, their landlord or landlady. Apparently, they'd been noise-sensitive from the very beginning, and David and Margaret had spent a lot of time concentrating on making sure that they didn't ring the bell too late or shut their door too enthusiastically, but none of this really came out in the classroom until they got in trouble for boiling the kettle too loudly. I think by that point Margaret was starting to feel that if this was how her ancestors behaved, she wasn't so keen to get in touch with them after all – it came out in a rush at the start of one particular day, that they had boiled their kettle too loudly.

'How do you boil a kettle too loudly?' someone asked.

'Well I don't know,' Margaret answered, a little wildly. 'This isn't some traditional thing, is it? I mean, in America people would think you were a little *odd* if you complained about the noise of a kettle boiling.' She was looking around slightly suspiciously, as if she thought perhaps we all secretly agreed that it was rather rude of her to go around boiling kettles in her flat. We tried to reassure her, but it wouldn't surprise me at all if she still feels a sense of relief every time she boils a kettle at home, away from the lunatic fringe of Aberystwyth. That's the landlord and landlady I'm referring to there, by the way, not the rest of the people on the course.

The best thing about Margaret and David, though, even including their faithful devotion to practice sessions in the Cŵps, was their fierce determination to speak Welsh as close to all the time as humanly possible. Forget about slipping into English in the class, I made the mistake of using an English word at coffee time once (probably something entirely innocent like 'lot', and I'll blame Kitty for that just one more time), and the look on Margaret's face made me worry that I might need a professional taster to check my pint in the Cŵps that night. On more than one occasion, I honestly thought that Margaret was going to start shouting at a *tutor* for switching into English, and you just have to love that kind of focus. I think she felt left out that no-one had invited her to go burning holiday homes and estate agents in the 80s.

Still, there was far less for her to get angry about while Heulwen was teaching us. It's amazing how little English gets used in class if a tutor makes it really clear that they are not in favour of 'the thin language'. I don't know – you read about how the Cymry Cymraeg are too quick to switch into English, and don't support learners enough, but I think anyone who says that has got a fair amount of cheek if they don't admit that it's a deeply natural urge for learners to switch back into English. And let's be honest, if you're going to switch back into English in the most supportive language learning environment you're ever going to encounter, where people are actively delighted if you pause to remember a word (because it gives them a chance to catch up and let their brains rest), how are you ever going to learn to stand your ground in the middle of a Welsh-speaking pub?

Heulwen week ended with our very own Prynhawn Llawen, on the Friday afternoon. We couldn't have a Noson Lawen, because there were some people leaving in the afternoon, and the point was to get all the different classes together – 1A, 1B, 2A, 2B and the worryingly fluent 3, the group that everybody tried very hard to avoid for obvious reasons. Our sketch was meant to be some kind of a knock-out competition for learning Welsh, with Heulwen the mocking judge who voted one of us off at the end of each round. I'm sure it must have been a relief for her to be able to stop being polite to us. Giles, I think, won – he turned out to have a gift of comic timing for his recitation of the sentence 'Rydw i'n meddwl taw Richard *Burton* yw e', which is one of those Wlpan sentences that you never forget, and, surprisingly enough, never actually need to use.

Class 3 did a sketch that was obviously very cleverly worked out, very witty, and very well received by the tutors. Unfortunately, none of the rest of us understood a word of it, and we were all far too nervous to ask any of them to explain it afterwards. Good learners, who sound as though they speak Welsh, are really quite hard to stomach for the rest of us. Do I sound bitter and twisted? It's okay, that's a natural part of the process.

Anyway, it's about time for the sex, isn't it? But I'm afraid to say that there wasn't any in Week Three. Well, not as far as I know, but then again I am usually one of the last to find out, let alone get involved. But Week Four, now that was a scorcher. Go on, turn the page.

Some Sex and a Hill

Pennod 7 – Cyffur yr Iaith Fain

The last week of an intensive residential course is a strange time. That is, even stranger than the rest of the course. People begin to remember that they have a life outside the classroom and the Cŵps, and, as the week goes on, more and more of them leave, because they've run out of holiday time. It's a bit depressing, to be honest – just when you've got used to everyone's different ways of doing things, and have grown genuinely close to some of them, you're all on the verge of going your separate ways. Sure, you swap email addresses, but you know that the chances are pretty high that what you're really saying is 'Goodbye, and have a good life.'

On the bright side, though, you've had your neurons fairly comprehensively re-wired by the fourth week, and you're actually getting used to spending your free time talking Welsh. Your brain is a bit too tired for you to realise it very clearly, but you have just acquired a new language, and if there was anywhere left in the world where people spoke Welsh and didn't understand English, you'd be okay. You might not get a reputation for being the most sparkling conversationalist, but you'd be okay.

That's an important point, actually – it's very easy for learners to get caught up in the whole thing about 'not being fluent', but fluent is such a vague word. Once someone has enough Welsh to cope with all the ordinary bits and pieces of a normal day, that's a valuable kind of fluency. From then on, all that matters is how often they have the chance to use their Welsh (and how often they choose to), and there's an easy solution to that. Move to Patagonia. Because, of course, hard though it is for the English (and many Welsh) to accept, there is somewhere that some people speak Welsh and don't understand English. Which is a staggering, but wonderful, thought. Not very practical, though, to expect all Welsh learners to move to Patagonia for five years after their first Wlpan course. There is another option, fortunately, which I'll explain later on.

Back on the emotional roller-coaster of Week Four, we had another new tutor, and I'd have to say that there can't be many more difficult things to do in the world of teaching than come in for the last week of a full-time course. I felt sorry for Joel even before he arrived – it was clear that several of us just didn't have the psychological energy left to get enthusiastic about a new tutor, but fair play to the man, he didn't let that stop him. I'm not sure if Joel had taught adult classes before, but he had that shining conviction of the new teacher about him, and had obviously not even considered the possibility that any of us might be lazy enough to want to speak any English at all in our last week.

He wouldn't even translate words for us that we didn't know, which was... well, entertaining. If we asked what something meant, he'd start by looking at us and repeating the word, as if enough patience from him would bring us to a sudden, intuitive understanding. Then, if we looked upset enough, or began to mutter threateningly under our breath, he would begin acting, and I can safely say that I will never, in my entire life, forget that the word 'cwympo' means to fall over. He just did it so *suddenly*, with such *conviction*, as if he'd been shot. I'm fairly sure he must have hurt himself, too, because he did it several times, just to make sure we'd understood. Either that, or 'cwympo' means something completely different, and Joel just had exceptionally bad balance.

The other important thing about the last week was something that didn't happen. You see, I'd promised myself that when I could speak Welsh, I would have a tattoo of y Ddraig Goch as a kind of painful present to myself. Let me put this into context – I'm not a tattoo sort of person, not least because needles make me faint, and my pain threshold is, well, low. Okay, okay, I'm a wimp, put it like that. But I'd decided that learning Welsh was such an important part of my life, of filling the identity gap which I'd always had, that I would celebrate it by a brief demonstration of courage. And I felt I would have earned my own, permanent Welsh dragon.

So fairly early on in the last week, I decided that I couldn't speak Welsh properly yet. It's that fluency thing again, you see – it's so much easier to concentrate on what you can't say, and what you don't understand, than it is to realise how much you have learnt. Besides, needles give me the horrors, so if it was a choice (as I had decided it was) between having a tattoo or coming back for another course the next year, there was no competition.

That's my elaborate excuse, anyway, and I'm sticking to it.

Apart from falling over a lot, Joel also played us songs. From a tape recorder, that is, rather than live – I don't think he could have played guitar at the same time as falling over. This went down very well with me, because I approved of his taste in music, even though one or two of the older members of the class were less enthusiastic. That was the first time I heard the music of Meic Stevens, so I've a fairly serious debt to Joel. I'd never heard of Meic Stevens before, although I've always been something of a music addict – he's another one of those cultural blind spots for non-Welsh speakers. It still amazes me how two cultures can co-exist side by side, and one of them can be so completely unaware of the other. Most Welsh speakers I know would find it almost impossible to imagine anyone living in Cymru who didn't know who Meic Stevens is, but for most non-Welsh speakers, his name would mean nothing. It is one of the most damagingly wrong things about the country that Cymru has become that it is so easy for people to live here without ever being made aware of the 'other' language, the 'other' culture. It sometimes seems almost impossible to believe the depth of ignorance of all things to do with Welsh that exists among those who have lost the language.

Let me give you a shameful example. I was living in Aberystwyth in 1992, when the National Eisteddfod hit town. No, living in Aberystwyth isn't the shameful bit. This is: I didn't hear about it. I didn't notice it was happening. If the English-language media paid the attention to Welsh-language culture that it ought to, that would not be possible. And it should not be possible.

In fact, quite a lot of Joel's classes seemed to trigger a political response in me. Maybe it was just a very emotional week, for the reasons I've already referred to, but by that point I was starting to feel overwhelmed by the realisation that I was beginning to speak the language that should by rights have been mine from birth.

Yes, okay, let me just climb back down from this soapbox. One evening during the last week, we had a concert by Robin Huw Bowen, the harpist. The effort that goes into arranging the evening entertainment on these courses, and the willingness of talented and successful musicians to give their time for free because it's for learners really drives home how passionate people are about this language. In fact, that passion is a key thing in the whole language question, and it's yet another point on my list of things to come back to later on. Whether you want me to or not…

Now, Robin Huw Bowen is a startlingly gifted harpist, but as far as I was concerned there turned out to be something even more important about him. Part way through the performance, chatting as he does between pieces, he revealed that he was a learner. It's always difficult to trust that kind of revelation, because lots of people who started learning Welsh when they were nine or ten and are entirely, utterly fluent are still likely to claim that they 'learnt' Welsh. But when you do meet someone who a) clearly speaks Welsh perfectly and b) appears to be claiming that they learnt it as an adult, you cannot help but be inspired. And to hope that maybe, just maybe, it might be possible for you, too, in the end.

(Of course, you also feel quite bitter and jealous at the same time, but that's what the Cŵps is for. Drown those sorrows. In Welsh.)

Internationally renowned harpist, Welsh learner – and gifted marketer, too. I'd never been much of a fan of the harp, to be honest, but even I felt that it would have been rude not to buy one of the CDs. He'd played superbly, of course, but even more than that, he'd spoken slowly enough for most of us to understand most of what he said. You have to repay that kind of helping hand.

And the week wore away, and the class got smaller and smaller – we had lost Anna at the weekend (she'd never really been the same after Rob left), and then Dafydd and Margaret left, and Kitty and Giles, and it all started to seem a bit of a ghostly experience in the classroom. What's more, those of us who were left had fairly comprehensively frazzled brains, and the prospect of lots of one-on-one time was not so much helpful as just frightening.

But Joel kept bouncing around the room enthusiastically, and falling over randomly, and trying to act out words like 'strategy' (you try it), and there was something in me that just didn't want the week to end. You're wrapped away from the world so comprehensively on an intensive course that the prospect of having to go back out into it is like waking up on a bitterly cold morning when it's still dark outside. You don't want to, it's too much effort, and not warm enough.

I was starting to remember that I was still in the middle of feeling broken-hearted, which had all vanished to an amazing degree while I was being overwhelmed by dozens of new Welsh words every day. I even felt as though none of it had really happened when I was speaking Welsh – that this whole idea of me as a Welsh speaker was such a new thing that I couldn't remember anything from before it, not when I was actually speaking Welsh. Now if I could just package that and sell it – broken heart? No problems, here's a sure fix – get rid of the language you were dumped in, and learn a brand new one! Ta-daa! Brand new heart, not a mark on it, good as new. Low mileage.

And it was round about then that it dawned on me that I did actually want to leave English behind.

In other words, that learning Welsh was more than just a hobby – it was the language I wanted to spend the rest of my life in, and I had seen for the first time that there were plenty of people doing exactly that. If it was good enough for them (and for two thousand years of poets and kings and saints), it was more than good enough for me. And English, rather to my surprise, had just turned out not to be all that *necessary* after all – something which very few English speakers seem to be able to swallow, and which too many Welsh speakers still don't really believe.

It's as though English is a drug, drawing people in with bright lights and parties splashed all over in wild colours, with films and television and bands and newspapers and all the media junk of the MUST have it NOW society – but in the morning, or whenever it wears off, you wake up huddled beneath a flyover in the dead part of town, with your feet in the gutter and your shoes lost and your face bruised and you hope it's only rain dripping down the wall. And your culture and heritage and ancestors have been zipped up in the black bodybag you can see floating down the grimy, scum-frothed canal.

Just say no. Just say no to a template world, where we all wear the same clothes and buy the same burgers and live in the same blocks of flats and of course speak the same language. Or, if you're starting to see how you can escape the ordinary and live a life more beautiful, just say 'Na!' And, if you're the confident type, 'Dim diolch.'

***

And then it was over. We'd had the last lesson, and we'd said goodbye, and we were sent uncertainly back out into what had been our lives, to try and make sense of how this new part of us fitted into who we used to be. The defining moment, I think, is at the end of your first intensive course – something in you knows that either that's it, you'll play around with the language, and come back to visit it from time to time, or, more unsettlingly and perhaps even more threateningly and certainly more excitingly, you realise that this isn't enough. You need more. You've learnt that you can detox from English, and get addicted to the language of heaven instead. You know it makes sense.

What? There was meant to be something about sex in that chapter? No, no, when I said scorcher, I meant politically speaking. But you might be pleasantly surprised in the next chapter. In fact, maybe you should go and get a cup of tea now, just to calm you down in advance.

Some Sex and a Hill

Some Sex and a Hill

Pennod 8 – I fyny yn y Fro Gymraeg

There are a number of different ways in which you can build on the really significant head start that an intensive, four-week Wlpan course gives you. You are, by this stage, genuinely capable of getting through all normal, day-to-day transactions in Welsh – you just need the determination to keep at it, however slow it makes you feel. At this point, every sentence you say is a step towards real, long-term success.

So, as I say, you can choose to build on this in several different ways. You can make sure that you let all your friends know that you are trying to speak Welsh whenever you can, and you will probably be surprised to discover that some of them are Welsh speakers. Well, unless you live in America, in which case I'd have to admit the chances are probably a little lower.

Alternatively, and with your heart in your teeth, you can get out there and actively hunt down some Welsh speakers, and make them your friends (whether they really want you to or not). Again, trickier in America, but entirely possible anywhere in Cymru. That's right – wherever you live in Cymru, you are not far away from a natural, fluent, first-language Welsh speaker. They just do far too good a job of keeping quiet about it, most of the time. Even in Cardiff, Welsh speakers are now at about 10% – think about it. In a city the size of Cardiff, that is a hell of a lot of Welsh speakers. And if you do make the effort to develop a new set of Welsh-speaking friends, you will be rewarded by genuine appreciation and a fast-track pass into the whole new culture that you've earned yourself. Don't believe the old lies about Welsh speakers being rude to learners – they're just not true. Admittedly, it's not always easy having to talk to someone in a language they're learning when you know you speak their language much better than they speak yours, but if you stick to your guns when a Welsh speaker switches into English, they'll switch back into Welsh. They don't use English because they think you're no good, they use English because they have been trained (by education, by the rubbish the newspapers print, by the lies some politicians tell) to believe that it's rude to speak Welsh to anyone who isn't fluent.

Finally, and perhaps a little more dramatically, you can choose to move to live somewhere where the majority of the population speak Welsh. In other words, Ynys Môn, Gwynedd or Ceredigion. (But you'd better hurry – while the Assembly is congratulating itself on the increase of learners in the south east, the natural heartlands of the language are under increasing pressure. Wait ten years, and it might be too late.)

Like the intelligent, committed Welsh learner I would like people to believe I am, of course, I did none of these.

No.

I moved to England.

And while you're still beginning to sneer, let me qualify that. I moved to *Essex*. Now, between you and me, Essex is not exactly a hotspot for Welsh language use. They pretty much finished killing off the last few stragglers a good fifteen hundred years ago.

Oh, you think I ought to have an excuse for such a bizarre piece of behaviour? Well luckily enough, it just so happens that I do, freshly woven. It was all my brother's fault, you see (a sentence which has been coming in useful for the last forty years or so). He's a doctor, with the Army, and was stationed in Colchester, and when I came out of the comfortable cocoon of Wlpan and realised that I had staggered all the way into a world in which I not only didn't have a fiancée, I also didn't have a job or a place to live, he offered me sanctuary.

I knew it was going to be a touch on the weird side the first time I walked into a newsagents' and had taken the breath to say 'Bore da' before realising that, well, I was in foreign parts. Talk about culture shock – I mean, really, it was at least another month before the Welsh words stopped trying to queue-barge their way to the front of my mouth every time I spoke to anyone. And I never really did stop saying 'Diolch', because I'm a well-brought-up boy (no, honestly), and 'Diolch' has always been part of the family vocabulary, in the way in which traces of the language survive even in pockets of otherwise English-speaking communities in parts of Cymru. The good folk of Essex probably thought I was lapsing into German, or Arabic, or any of the many languages that they are more familiar with than they are with Welsh.

Stop and think about that for a moment – is it just me, or is it a totally incredible, as in literally unbelievable, thing that the people of England should be so much more likely to recognise French or German than the other living, kicking language that shares this peculiar political mass they like to call Englandandwales? All sorts of foreign languages and cultures are taught (and rightly so) in the schools of England, to help the children learn more about the world in which they live – but nothing, absolutely *nothing* is done to teach them about the other languages and cultures on the very same island on which they live. I mean, anyone can see that is wrong – can't they?

So, there I was in deepest darkest Essex, where the natives looked restless if I spoke Welsh to them, and all I had to keep myself pure was my comprehensive set of Wlpan tapes, and a copy of Gareth King's 'Colloquial Welsh'. Oh, and the internet. So that's a big, heartfelt thank you to Wlpan for producing the tapes, to Mr King for writing what is possibly the only book you need to work through if you want a conversational grasp of the language, and to Bill Gates. Not many people think of Bill Gates as someone lending a helping hand in the Welsh language's battle for survival, but he is – or he can be, if we're creative enough about what he's helped bring into existence.

In fact, it was email more than the internet that was important, because it allowed me to keep in touch with Haf – she patiently answered even my most confused and confusing emails, and regularly encouraged me with warm words of praise, such as 'I can usually understand most of what you write.' What more could anyone ask for? And above the simple matter of practice, her emails also kept me aware of the fact that Welsh had not stopped existing as a language once I walked out of the university accommodation on the last day of the Wlpan course (after checking the cupboards carefully to see if there were any leftover packets of pizza base mix). This, in turn, kept me aware of the fact that I had made a decision – that I wanted the language on a full-time, for-real basis, and although my plans weren't exactly clear when I first arrived at my brother's tiny house (do some freelance work, feel sorry for myself, listen to music, learn how to build web sites, and feel sorry for myself), the fact that the language had become a priority for me was already beginning to shape the decisions that I was going to make over the course of the next few months.

That, and one other thing. It was Haf who had first suggested it – 'If you want to hear Welsh around you all the time, you need to move up to the North.'

By which she did *not* mean Essex.

Move up to the North. It had a kind of ring to it, and it stuck in my head as I wandered in and out of various shops in Essex where, time and again, it turned out to my surprise that no-one spoke Welsh. In fact, on one memorable occasion, my brother and I stopped at a chippy in Colchester and discovered that the man serving the chips came from Kosovo, where my brother had served with the UN forces. Keen to be friendly, my brother trotted out his few phrases of Serbian, and (since he fortunately wasn't

Albanian) the gentlemen behind the counter responded enthusiastically with more Serbian than you could comfortably shake a stick at (and far too much for the brother to cope with). Meanwhile, I stood bilingually useless in the background, thinking what an insane world it is when you have more chance of practising Serbian in Essex than you have of talking Welsh. I mean damn it, we're next door neighbours. But neighbourly feeling between the indigenous cultures in the British Isles is not all it ought to be, whichever way you slice the cake.

Move up to the North. My Taid came from Garn Fadryn in Pen Llŷn, so it ought to have felt quite automatic. But the only area of Cymru I knew with any sense of belonging was the Aberystwyth to Machynlleth stretch, coupled with faint but emotive memories of Cwm Cynllwyd. I must have been up to the North before, but it would have been when the mother and the brother were insisting on going climbing, and I've always been very much an armchair climber. As in, mountains look beautiful, and as far as I'm concerned, if you climb up to the tops of the damned things, you can't *see* them any more. That's okay, I'll look after the car and/or drive round to meet you on the other side if you'd like. Appealing to the selfish side of the more Neanderthal, 'it's there so we've got to go up it' members of the family usually got me off the hook. Net result, I never really took any notice whatsoever of where we actually were.

Move up to the North. It had bedded itself down so successfully in the back of my head that eventually, without having got over the qualms of not knowing the first thing about Gogledd Cymru, I accepted the fact that I was going to go and live there. Where precisely? Well, Porthmadog.

No, I'm still not a hundred percent sure why myself, except for the fact that it looked sort of convenient on the map (thank you, yes, I've learnt that lesson), and the Glaslyn valley is one of the most beautiful places on the face of the earth.

My mother didn't think these were very good reasons for deciding where I was going to live, and when I announced my intention of taking a lift up to Port with my brother when he was off on one of his climbing malarkeys, so that I could spend the day sorting out somewhere to live, and get a lift back down with him, she became frankly abusive. She explained that I was devoid of any intelligence and that no-one can walk into a town and find a place to live on the same day, and that I was probably destined to be homeless, shiftless and feckless for the rest of my days.

Two out of three ain't bad, as the song goes. In fact, I'd found a flat in Port within the first half hour after my brother dropped me off, by looking in the windows of three newsagents, making one phone call, and strolling round to have a look at the place. It wasn't the last word in luxury, but I wasn't the last word in wealth, and it offered all I needed – a fair-sized living room, and a bedroom, bathroom and kitchenette. What's more, the landlord and landlady were friendly, and the landlady spoke Welsh – off to a good start, I thought smugly to myself.

Once I'd agreed terms and dates, I went off to kill the rest of the day in the Sportsman's, or Yr Heliwr, as I conscientiously tried to think of it. And looking back on it, I then did one of the more brave things that I have managed in my life to date – I started talking to the old men at the bar. In Welsh.

The main thanks for that must go to the Wlpan course, for teaching me that a permanent sense of embarrassment is a healthy part of the process of learning a new language, and also to Haf, who had more or less convinced me that everyone in the North spoke Welsh. Oddly enough, I didn't have to grit my teeth, or spend time psyching myself up, before saying 'Helo' (see how naturally I've learnt to leave that unnecessary second 'l' out?) – it just seemed the obvious thing to do.

And it was immediately worthwhile. Okay, the one mildly drunk old bloke who talked to me solidly for the next three or four hours didn't actually seem to understand a lot of what I was saying, but that didn't matter – put it like this, he wasn't exactly *dependent* on my contributions. He had the conversation under control as it was. And no, if I'm honest, I didn't understand a great deal of what *he* said, but (and this made me feel very good about myself) I did understand a fair bit more than I had really been expecting. In fact, I might even have understood almost as much as I would have from a mildly drunk, speech-blurred, rambling and English-speaking old man. Hard to be sure – I'd never have sat and listened to a drunk old Englishman for that long. It just wouldn't have had the same attraction.

By the time my brother had turned up again, something in the mildly smoky room (and possibly in the three or four pints I'd invested in, on the grounds that alcohol helps me speak Welsh better) had left me feeling entirely certain that I had made the right decision – that Porthmadog was going to be the right place for me, at least for the time being. In a way, I suppose you could choose to pinpoint that afternoon as the day I arrived home. I still had a fair amount of journeying to do, but I was home.

That's one of the odder things about recapturing the language that's part of your lost heritage – miles from anywhere you can remember being before, miles from anyone you know, you can quite suddenly feel strangely but distinctly at home. Maybe it's something in the blood – or maybe it's the weight lifting off your shoulders because you know you're not going to have to say, 'I'm sorry, I don't speak Welsh.'

The last month I had left with my brother before moving up to Port in the beginning of the new year was spent buried in 'Colloquial Welsh' and going through my Wlpan notes in an increasingly fretful sort of way. Once I'd left Port, you see, I started to feel quite nervous about going back. It was as though, having made the decision, having gone past the point of no return, I was beginning to realise that there was a very serious change to my life ahead of me. It had all seemed to flow quite naturally up until that point, none of it had needed much thought – and now there it was, cut and dried, and nothing for it but to carry on. It reminded me a little of arriving in Zimbabwe several years before, to start a two-year posting – the plane settling down to Harare airport, the veldt stretching out in the bright sunshine, and me sitting there thinking 'Wait a moment – when *exactly* did I agree to do this?'

January 1st, 2001. Unpacking some of my things, and leaving others in the boxes they would have to stay in until I found somewhere with a bit more room. Shifting some of the furniture around almost absent-mindedly, for no particular reason. I'd landed again, and I felt lost and at home at the same time. In

Zimbabwe, there was no pressure, in some ways, because it was obvious I didn't come from there. In Porthmadog, I felt as though it was wrong of me not to belong more already. I think perhaps I was noticing the fact that I had spent the last ten years quietly letting my country down, by being part of the flow of young people away from the rural heartlands where they are so desperately needed. But there was, at least, one thing that counted in my favour – I could speak enough Welsh to get by. I wasn't going to be responsible for forcing anyone to speak English. As far as that went, part of me already *did* belong.

Some Sex and a Hill

Some Sex and a Hill

Pennod 9 – Cana dy Gân

I did two things almost immediately in Port, and both of them turned out to be very important. Only one of them was deliberate – the other was a complete accident, which shows how little I have tended to deserve the good fortune that has come my way.

First of all, I signed up for a Welsh course – three sessions a week, two hours a session. I knew that I needed the discipline, and part of me just wanted the emotional support. I had a tricky decision to make straight away – the next course after Wlpan is Uwch ('Higher' – which already sounded a bit ambitious to me), and the only available 'Cwrs Uwch' was across the Cob in Penrhyndeudraeth. 'Across the Cob' in Porthmadog has the same ring to it as when other people in other places say 'Overseas' or 'Australia'. And I didn't have a car. But there was a course being held in Port itself – a Cwrs Pellach. So here's my problem – I'm a nervous type, and 'Further' than 'Higher' was just starting to sound quite dizzying to

95

me. I didn't feel ready to be any further or higher than I absolutely had to be, and given the choice, I would have been keen to get back into the comfortable embrace of the initial Wlpan course itself, with Ffred and Sandra and their dog Bendigeidfran, whose name I could now almost pronounce. Could we maybe just pretend that we were doing the Pellach, and secretly take the short cut back to Wlpan?

No, it turned out, we couldn't. Eleri, my tutor to be, had already decided that I sounded as though I'd fit in better in the Cwrs Pellach than I would in Uwch – Welsh tutors are always far too ready to think you're better than you actually are, in my experience. And having an accent which just sounds strange, instead of strange and English, helps them to make the mistake. Mind you, learners are so good at thinking they are much worse than they really are, tutors probably know they need to overcompensate in the other direction.

Gritting my teeth and not looking forward to being the most stupid in the class, I joined up, and started to get myself back into the habit. I don't think it was my first lesson, but it might well have been either my second or third, when I made my mistake. You can put it down to over-enthusiasm, if you're kind (or stupidity, if you're not). Gwyn, under pressure to say something to introduce himself (so maybe it was my first lesson, actually), came out with 'Rydw i'n aelod o Gôr.'

It turns out that pride really does come before a fall. One of the last things we'd worked on in the Wlpan course had been the conditional, and I realised with a slight rush to the head that I knew how to say 'I wouldn't mind joining a choir.'

'Fyswn i ddim yn meindio ymaelodi â chôr,' I contributed shyly, hoping I'd earn a metaphorical pat on the head from Eleri for saying something, and perhaps getting some of it correct. Instead, I got Gwyn turning to look at me, and saying cheerfully, 'We've got a practice tonight – why don't you come along?'

Well, let's forgive him for lapsing into English for a moment, and consider instead the full impact of this particular suggestion. I am, not to put too fine a point on it, less than naturally gifted with musical talents. I am, in fact, the resident family black sheep when it comes to music. My brother was an outstanding treble, and played violin and cello, and my mother was what's always sounded to me like a *frighteningly* strong soprano (particularly when you're trying to have a lie-in) and also played piano. Me? Well, when the ten-year-old me failed to break his recorder by leaving it in the road for lorries to run over (bloody tough things, these plastic recorders, I can tell you), it was left to my mother to suggest that perhaps I didn't need to practise very *often*. Not within a mile or two of the house, anyway.

And singing? Well, I've always wanted to be able to sing. And I tend to sing enthusiastically if left to myself in a shower. But, unfortunately, these two character elements do not necessarily add up to someone who *can* sing. In fact, they don't add up at *all* to someone who can sing. In fact, they mostly add up in my case to someone who is wise if they 'sing' only in private, and preferably out of earshot of any family pets, which experience has told me can be easily frightened.

So that was the musical background against which Gwyn was suggesting I came along to the choir, and against which, at about half-past seven that evening, I found myself sneaking up to the church and hoping whole-heartedly that it would turn out to be the wrong night, and I could make a quick, badly tuned getaway.

But no. On the contrary – I was a touch on the early side, and the conductor had time to give me what he calmly referred to as a 'quick voice test'. Maybe it will reveal the depths of my musical stupidity if I admit to you the embarrassing fact that it hadn't crossed my mind that I might have to have a voice test. I'd just thought innocently that I would be able to sing very, very quietly, or in fact *mime*. But you can't mime in a voice test, can you? (Well, I tried to begin with, but he was having none of it.) It was so unfair – I mean, asking someone like me to have a voice test is like asking a fish to take a quick cycling proficiency exam. And I think I may well have gawped at our conductor in quite a goldfish-like manner too, just to drive the point home.

Ah. You've noticed that I refer to him as 'our' conductor. No, I can't explain how I got through the voice test, unless it possibly had something to do with the fact that the choir were cripplingly short of singers and he'd decided that they could always shoot me later.

Apart from the inevitable impact on the overall sound of the choir, though, my membership (£1 a week, or £10 a go if you tend to forget for more than a couple of months in a row, as I do) was a stroke of complete brilliance in terms of my continuing journey towards the tempting horizon over which the Welsh language kept disappearing. No-one in the choir ever tried to speak English to me, even though I was obviously pretty incoherent in Welsh, and the 'quick pint' or two or three after our weekly practice was priceless. I relaxed enough to talk a little more once the first intake of alcohol kicked in, and I got to listen to Welsh in its most natural, utterly unselfconscious form.

In other words, I didn't understand a *word*. Not for *months*. I just nodded and smiled a lot, and looked the other way if something sounded like a question. And that pretty much sums up the first six months or so of my social life in Porthmadog – I refused to speak English and I couldn't really speak Welsh, but I was quite happy to get quietly drunk in a corner while this language that I was growing to love so much was breaking over me like a heavy sea.

And, of course, every incomprehensible sentence was dragging me slowly but surely towards the land. There are times, when you're learning a language that you really intend to speak full-time, when you just have to give up, and go with the flow. I was still doing my gwaith cartref conscientiously for the Cwrs Uwch, but the days of sitting down and trying to memorise long lists of vocabulary were gone. Some people call them plateaus – those times when all your work doesn't seem to be making you any better, and if you don't care enough about the language, you sulk, and give in.

If you ever feel like that about Welsh, all you have to do is spend more time in a pub. Really. (Well, it does need to be a mostly Welsh-speaking one, naturally enough.) Give in for a few months, forget about trying to speak, and just let it all crash over your head again and again and again until you have the sudden shock of realising that you've just understood the latest piece of gossip or a particularly filthy joke. And if you're stuck for Welsh-speaking pubs, just join a Male Voice Choir (er, unless you're not qualified, in terms of being, well... not Male. If it's any help to you, I'm led to believe there are such things as Mixed Choirs, which accept people of the female persuasion, although that's always sounded a bit racey to me). They'll help you find at least a corner of a pub where you can drown in the language as well as in the spilt beer.

It's just about the perfect combination – a chance to go out drinking in the language (as it were) together with regular lessons. I enjoyed the stroll out to the CYMAD building on the industrial estate, where our classes were held, particularly when the early spring sun would hammer a thin layer of gold over the fields and rocky outcrops and the broad expanse of Moelwyn Fach, Moelwyn Fawr and Cnicht, the roll of the names seeming ever more natural and familiar to me. Sometimes I would catch myself remembering that I had a broken heart, but mostly I was buoyed up by the sense that I had arrived somewhere real, and had finally stopped pretending to myself that it was okay that I couldn't speak Welsh.

What's more, by this stage my life was being enriched by 'Pobol y Cwm', much to the concern of my Welsh-speaking friends. They couldn't seem to grasp that however much they grumbled about it being just another typically rubbish soap opera, I remained addicted. Of course, for me it was still so comparatively rare to understand an entire *sentence* that the likelihood of me starting to judge the dramatic flow was minimal, to say the least. I tried as hard as I could to watch every episode during the week, because if I had to watch the subtitled version on Sundays, I knew I would just end up reading them instead of listening properly. It wasn't exactly helping me acquire a more northern accent, needless to say, but at least I was now aware of the danger, and determined not to pick up any of this 'Sa i'n gwybod' business. Even now, I've got a soft spot for 'Pobol y Cwm' – I hardly ever watch it any more, but I'll always be grateful for the role it played in my attempts to use and understand the language more naturally.

Inspired, perhaps, by 'Pobol y Cwm', I even signed up for an extra lesson in Porthmadog – well, a 'Sgwrs a Stori' group that met for a couple of hours every other week, where the main point was to chat, swap gossip, and have occasional speakers come in to give talks to us about pretty much anything, as long as it was in Welsh. The presentations would usually follow the same kind of pattern – the speaker would start out very conscious that they were talking to learners, and would speak clearly, and quite slowly, and then the more involved they got with their subject, the less they would remember that we were learners, and the more naturally they would talk. It worked the same way for us, too – we'd start by concentrating desperately and trying to work out every sentence, and then we'd get distracted by the subject matter, and realise forty minutes later that we'd been understanding a lecture in Welsh without thinking about it. I think the 'Sgwrs a Stori' courses are possibly the most effective part of the entire process of Welsh adult education, and that's saying a lot, because I think that (despite the pitiful under-funding) the second-language adult education system in Cymru is amongst the very best in the world.

If that sounds like a bit of an exaggeration, here's some background for you. I've had a go at learning a number of different languages – I studied the majority language, Shona, for two years while I was in Zimbabwe, I've studied Arabic in Dubai and Egypt, I've studied Thai using a combination of English-developed coursework and visits to villages in northern Thailand, and I've studied Italian. In not one of them have I achieved anything like the conversational ability that the Welsh system has given me. The Arabic is a particularly worthwhile example – I spent over three years working hard on my Arabic, including a four-week immersion course in Cairo one hot, grimy summer, but it simply never became a conversational language for me. What's more, I've dabbled in quite a few other languages through a number of different systems, including trying to acquire bits and pieces of French, German, Dutch, Spanish and Afrikaans. I don't believe there is a language learning system or structure out there which is better than what we have right here in Cymru – which makes it all the more of an outrage that the Assembly underfunds it so scandalously. We should be holding it up proudly as a best practice model, and making it clear to everyone living in Cymru that the support is there to make the language available to them. But no – instead, budgets and jobs in the Welsh adult education sector get cut, and the Assembly talks proudly about its aim to create a bilingual Cymru. What a mockery.

The 'Sgwrs a Stori' classes turned out to be important to me for another reason. One morning, early in the spring of 2001, we were told that our next session was going to be about the wildlife and traditions of Ynys Enlli, the island of the thousand saints, off the furthestmost point of Pen Llŷn, and that the lecture would be presented by a Gwynedd County councillor called Seimon Glyn. Nobody in the group had the faintest idea of the storm that was brewing – a storm that was going to be large and ugly enough to need its own chapter.

Some Sex and a Hill

Some Sex and a Hill

Pennod 10 – Cariad at Iaith

It was clear in the early years of this century that a lot of people throughout Cymru had been lured by absurd newspaper stories (from such shining examples of journalistic integrity as the *Welsh Mirror*) into believing in Seimon Glyn as some kind of an English-baby-eating demon in barely human form, more likely to burn your house down than to say 'Hello' with two Ls, and quite probably plotting to rise up out of Pen Llŷn at the head of an army of pitchfork- and scythe-wielding murderers.

I've often wondered if the people who write malicious rubbish, and the people who believe it, would be shocked (or possibly even ashamed) if they could hear Seimon Glyn talk about Enlli. Remember, if you will, that no-one in our group had read the *Cymro* or the *Herald Cymraeg*, and that we didn't have a clue about a certain infamous radio interview that had been broadcast the week before our 'Sgwrs a Stori' session. What we heard, and what left an impression on every single one of us, English and Welsh alike, was a man who quite obviously loved Ynys Enlli with a real passion, to such an extent that not only was our class fired with a longing to visit the island ourselves, but we would also have paid good money to have had him back to speak to us again. Unfortunately, he turned out to be more than a little busy over the next few months.

Maybe I'm getting a touch out of my philosophical depth here, but as far as I can see, people are either motivated by love or by self-interest (or, in some unhappy cases, by hatred), and one of the most notable aspects of the drive to keep the Welsh language alive is the remarkably high percentage of people involved in it because they are driven by real, bone-deep love for their language.

It seems such a basic divide to me – look on the one hand at the ordinary, everyday individuals who volunteer to teach Welsh for free in their villages, who spend their time arranging pickets against rapacious estate agents, who help arrange concerts or Nosweithiau Llawen, and you will see people who are motivated by love. Look, on the other hand, at the politicians and journalists who descend to the use of mindless, negative repetition (and are paid to do so), who accuse people who care about Welsh of being inward, negative, hostile or narrow-minded – or racist – and ask yourself what their motives are.

If they are driven by love, then what exactly is it that they love?

No, love is never mentioned in their attacks on the language. It seems that some of them are motivated by political self-interest, and others by hatred and fear of something which they don't understand, and to which they refuse even to listen. I'm not sure which of the two is the more pitiful.

And so began the summer of the year 2001, with wild, bitter accusations being hurled at the head of a man I'd heard talk tenderly about the hedgebirds and butterflies of Enlli. I couldn't reconcile the two images, and it became the itch that drove me to start buying and reading the *Cymro* regularly. I needed to know what was going on here; I needed to know why such an obviously good person was being attacked so viciously. And, of course, I needed to practise for my TGAU – for my second language Welsh GCSE, at which it seemed like a good idea for me to be aiming. The whole political scene in Cymru was in uproar about the language again, and I was bobbling along in the middle of it all, increasingly concerned by the issues but delighted at every chance I got to practise.

And now for another slightly ashamed moment – for another example of the gulf in understanding and perception between the Cymry and the Cymry di-Gymraeg (just to digress for a moment, I think it is a rather odd thing that Welsh-speaking Welsh people are called Cymry Cymraeg – you wouldn't talk about 'French-speaking French', would you? It's the Cymry di-Gymraeg are the unusual element, so let them be Cymry di-Gymraeg – but the Cymry are just the Cymry, today every bit as much as they have been for most of the last two thousand years).

Back to my shame. When I started reading the articles about Seimon Glyn in the *Cymro* and the *Herald* was when I first learnt that the language was in real danger.

Does that seem hard to believe?

I won't make any excuses, but it might be useful for English and Welsh speakers alike to understand some of the patterns behind that kind of unawareness. Whenever I'd been living in Cymru, I'd always taken it for granted that everyone else could speak Welsh if they chose to, and that I was the odd one out. I know, I know – I also didn't have a real understanding that it was an all-day every-day language for anyone, but cultural blindness can leave you pretty confused. I didn't have a *clue* that it was really, genuinely in danger of dying out.

Yes, I read Welsh newspapers – but they were English language, and they presumed their (largely Welsh, albeit di-Gymraeg) audience could not possibly be interested in the language. And, of course, I knew that S4C had been won in 1980, and I walked past Siop y Pethe pretty much every time I was in Aberystwyth. It is so dangerously easy, from the outside, to think that everything is fine. This is one of the reasons why the work of groups like Cymdeithas yr Iaith is so enormously important – the language is part of the heritage of every single Welsh person, and those who can't speak it still need to be taught that it is in danger of being lost as a real, living, community language. If they don't even hear about the problems, how can they ever know that they need to help?

And that's an important question – because it is a very foolish mistake to presume that only Welsh speakers want to see the language flourish. A foolish mistake that a lot of politicians, unfortunately, seem capable of making on a regular basis. But the Cymry di-Gymraeg are not by definition against the language – they may feel defensive that they don't speak it themselves, they may be uncomfortable if Labour politicians try and peddle the old lie about Plaid Cymru wanting to force the language down everyone's throats, and some of them can even seem quite hostile towards the language, but look at the facts. More and more people who don't speak Welsh are sending their children to Welsh-medium schools;

in fact, there aren't enough places in Welsh-medium schools for all the children whose families want them to have the Welsh education that they themselves were denied.

So the Assembly is busy funding more Welsh-medium schools, right, to fulfil this real, encouraging, growing demand? Yes, sure they are – and that's a pig just flew past your window.

So something new was growing in me as a direct result of learning Welsh. I was becoming politicised, partly because it is not really possible to speak Welsh without making, willingly or unwillingly, a political statement. Add it to the list of unfair biases against Welsh speakers, if you will – it is almost impossible simply to live through the medium of Welsh because you'd rather, and that's an end to it. No – every time you start a conversation in Welsh, you are risking being considered aggressive, or anti-English, or a political activist, when all you want to do is lead an ordinary life in your own language. One experience from Porthmadog remains crystal clear in my memory – I was standing in the street just down from my flat, at about half-past ten in the evening, saying goodnight to a friend of mine, chatting across the roof of her car for a minute or two before she left. Suddenly, a window above us opened, and an overweight, middle-aged woman shoved her head out. 'What the hell d'you think you're doing?' she spat. 'It's the middle of the sodding night, you'll wake my dog up, people like you are so bloody ignorant.'

Charming, I thought to myself – what an elegant way to ask us to be quiet (not that we were being loud anyway, but hey). So I said, defensively, 'We're not talking that loudly, and it's not that late.'

But here's the thing – we had, of course, been talking in Welsh, so naturally enough I spoke to her in Welsh. And that's when it hit me – almost hissing with anger, she let her voice rise: 'I spoke to you in English, so you'll damned well answer me in English.'

The sheer arrogance of that leaves me speechless.

Forget how rude she was, forget how hostile and aggressive and generally unpleasant – what staggering arrogance it takes to *order* someone to speak English. Unfortunately, this is by no means a rare example of that particular attitude – Welsh speakers who take the step of starting conversations in Welsh get it, quite literally, all the time.

'Don't talk that stupid language with me...'
'I can't understand a word you're saying, mate!'
'What are you – German?'

If the Assembly are right that we can sit back and rely on the famous 'good will' they claim to have won for the language, why is it that so few people are capable of saying 'I'm sorry, I don't speak Welsh. Would you mind speaking English?' Is simple politeness too much to ask as an example of this 'good will' we hear so much about?

Come to think of it, how hard would it be for anyone with genuine good will towards Welsh to learn how to say 'Mae'n ddrwg gen i, dw i ddim yn siarad Cymraeg'? How about it – if you don't speak Welsh, have a go at learning that sentence, and the next time someone speaks to you in Welsh, don't think that they're having a go – just bring out that single, polite sentence, and you'll be making a contribution towards building a better Cymru.

Of course, the more confident I became about using my Welsh, the more I discovered how hard it is, even in Gwynedd, to spend your whole time in the medium of Welsh. There are plenty of shop assistants in Porthmadog who don't speak Welsh (which strikes me as an amazing example of marketing stupidity), bus drivers who don't speak Welsh, business people who don't speak Welsh. Forget all this rubbish about how nobody's forced to speak English any more – it happens every day. Any Welsh speaker is forced to speak English on pretty much a daily basis, and as far as I was concerned, as well as being morally unacceptable, it was also a direct attack on my chances of getting an 'A' in my TGAU. Every person who couldn't speak Welsh with me was striking another blow against my exam hopes – I regularly felt like saying 'Look, for God's *sake*, I've got an exam coming up!'

As the TGAU got closer, and I began to panic about getting all my coursework in on time (in the end, the only reason that I managed to do the five-minute tape conversation was because Eleri kidnapped an innocent member of staff at CYMAD and forced her to talk to me for five minutes, which reveals my general levels of organisation), I became more and more determined to run away from anyone I heard speaking English. The problem, you see, is that your first language does not like being left behind, and it runs so deeply in your consciousness that a word or two of it overheard in a shop can snap you back into thinking in English just when you'd had a stream of thought going in Welsh.

It's something, I believe, that too many learners don't really 'get'. I couldn't begin to count how many times I've heard even quite advanced learners talking in English during a break for tea, or even during a class. Most tutors tend to let them get away with it, because they don't want to be accused of being heavy-handed, but the sheer fact of it is that if you are learning another language, any other language, it is much more likely that you will succeed if you stop speaking English. Not necessarily all the time, as I was trying to do (although it does make the process much faster), but at the very least while you are actually in the learning situation – classroom, pub, wherever it be. The simple truth is this – if you can't say something in Welsh, it will help you learn faster if you just don't say it, rather than lapsing back in English.

Honestly. I'm not being extreme here at all, far from it. It's a very well-established fact of language learning – often referred to as 'target language immersion'. If you keep talking your first language, you crowd out your new language, and your chances of speaking naturally and confidently take a nose-dive. As I almost said before – you'll learn more Welsh sitting silently in the corner of a Welsh-speaking pub than you will spending your time speaking English in the middle of Welsh classes.

All of which means that it is very sensible for you to learn the Welsh for 'How do you say [x] in Welsh?' extremely early on. *(Sut mae deud [x] yn y Gymraeg?)*

And all of which also means that when I arrived in Dolgellau for the exam itself, I was as edgy as the proverbial cat on hot bricks, because I knew that if any of my fellow examinees started talking in English, I was probably going to bite them. I was certainly going to have to run away at top speed before it had a negative effect on my careful exam preparations – I hadn't spoken to my mother for almost a week (apart from to say 'Helo! Wyt ti'n iawn? Iawn. Yndw, dw i'n iawn. Iawn. Nos da!'), and I'd been going out and getting drunk in Welsh with friends pretty much every night. Come to think of it, it was a bit of a surprise that I was in a sound enough physical condition to drive down to Dolgellau. But those are the kind of sacrifices you have to make if you want to learn Welsh. Are you starting to see the attraction?

Getting an 'A', of course, wasn't particularly important to me. I was only doing the exam to give me a focus, to force me not to skip too much of the grammar. It was something to help me concentrate, but it obviously wasn't going to make any actual difference to how well I did or didn't speak Welsh.

Those, at least, were the sentences I kept saying to myself (yes, in Welsh) driving across the open blue-green plain of Trawsfynydd and then dipping down into the sun-dappled forests on the way to Dolgellau. They were complete lies, of course – as I admitted before, I'm quite psychotically competitive, and part of me knew that if I didn't get an 'A', there was a fighting chance I'd emigrate again and go back to learning Thai instead.

In all honesty, I was surprised by how nervous I was about the exam. It really did feel like being back at school, but worse, because this time I knew that I really *had* been trying. I was going to take failure much more personally than I had ever done at school. And everyone else seemed quite nervous, too, which wasn't helpful – although at least no-one was speaking English. It's impossible to engage in much small talk before a Welsh exam – if you talk English, someone like me will start screaming, and if you talk Welsh too well everyone will feel threatened and even less confident than they already were. You have to settle for simple little statements about the weather, and if you're a real humanitarian, throw in the occasional deliberate error, so that people can hear it and think 'Hey! That was a mistake, and I noticed! Maybe I'm going to pass!'

The oral was the worst bit for me. It's as if you're stuck in some kind of vast echo chamber, or are being recorded with 'immediate playback' switched on – everything you say seems to drift past your ears a second or two after you've said it, so that you can think 'No! I didn't mean that! And I *do* know there's meant to be a soft mutation there!' And then if you're really unlucky, you get caught in the trap of trying to correct your mistakes, and then you're trying to correct the fresh mistakes that you made while you were trying to correct your initial mistakes, and then suddenly it's time over and you've spent half an hour trying to explain your name and where you come from. And on the way out, part of you wants to demand the examiner's home address, so that you can send her a letter explaining that you do honestly know that 'yn' causes a nasal mutation in place names, and to say that you want to throw yourself on the mercy of the court and would like her to take into consideration two and a half thousand other similar offences.

Once I'd survived the TGAU, I knew I was into difficult waters. It was summer, you see, and apart from taking in enough proofreading and copywriting work to pay for the rent, I wasn't very inclined to do anything much else. Summer and work have never seemed to me to go very well together – I'm sure I would have got better grades at school if the exams had all been in the winter, when it's much harder to skip lessons and go sunbathing with a good book instead. This might also explain why I never felt as if I got completely into my stride in all those years that I spent working in Dubai – too much sun. Look, it's a perfectly good excuse, leave it alone.

But I couldn't afford to ease up on the Welsh. No way – I had another Wlpan course looming on the horizon, and to make sure that I was ready for it, I'd booked into a two-week course at Bangor University just as a warm-up session. I had a nasty feeling, you see, that I'd spent too much time claiming to be learning Welsh by socialising in the local hostelries, and not enough actually getting down and dirty with grammar exercises. Not to put too fine a point on it, I felt uncomfortably close to having learnt Welsh well enough to consider myself illiterate in the language, which wasn't attractive, once I thought about it. I was hoping that Bangor could help solve that before I showed my face back down in Aberystwyth – little did I realise that the feelings of illiteracy were only going to get worse. And, of course, even more importantly, I hadn't stopped to consider the one obvious, major disadvantage to trying to learn Welsh in Bangor.

It's a heck of a long way to drive from the Hen Goleg in Bangor down to the Cŵps for a night out.

Some Sex and a Hill

Some Sex and a Hill

Pennod 11 – Dinas Ddysg

There's no getting away from it, a Welsh course (however intensive) where you go home at the end of the day's classes can't even begin to compare with one that has evening activities. It's as though you're stopping and starting all the time, and of course you don't get to know the other learners anything like as well. Having said that, though, the two weeks in Bangor were entertaining in their own way.

The best part for me was that Ann, our tutor, a short, lively, grey-haired and highly organised lady from Ynys Môn, placed a very high priority on telling us what words and sentences would actually sound like when real, live Welsh speakers were saying them. This was something that no-one else had offered me before, and it made an immediate difference. She explained, for example, that 'Mi fues i yn Llangefni' would come out as 'Sheen Llangefni' or thereabouts, and within the first week of these kinds of insider tips, I was starting to feel that I was understanding more of what people were saying as I eavesdropped on them in shops or on buses. That sort of confidence is a vital part of learning any language.

Once again, the class was made up out of what I was coming to learn was the usual mix of completely unexpected character types – it really is impossible to predict who you'll find in a class of Welsh learners, because there are so many different reasons for people to want to learn the language, and perhaps because more and more people are becoming aware of its importance. There was Steve, a Scottish astronomer who lived in Wrecsam and was learning Welsh on the impressive grounds that Wrecsam is in Cymru, and it would be rude to live in a country without learning the language. It's a healthy attitude, and it would be good to see it become the widespread norm. Steve had been working at his Welsh for quite a while, and was entirely capable of socialising through the medium of his new language (which, as you'll have guessed by now, is a key issue for me), so we were able to get the occasional pint in after classes in the Globe (which is almost an acceptable substitute for the Cŵps). My favourite memory of Steve is his story of having been flying out to Italy and absent-mindedly saying 'Diolch' to the airhostess with the drinks (I've told you, it's a very difficult thing to stop yourself). One of his fellow passengers heard this, and asked him, in Welsh, if he was from Cymru. It turned out that she, an Italian, had a Welsh boyfriend, and although she didn't have a word of English, she had a fair amount of Welsh. Which turned out to be particularly important when they arrived in Italy and Steve's luggage was lost, because he couldn't speak any Italian, and none of the relevant staff had any English.

So somewhere in the depths of Italy, an Italian and a Scot worked out what had happened to his luggage through the medium of Welsh. And some people have the cheek to say that Welsh isn't a 'relevant', modern language!

The Bangor fortnight was also where I met my first live Welsh speaker from the Wladfa – Patagonia, the Welsh-speaking part of Argentina, where the numbers of Welsh learners have been steadily increasing in the last twenty years (and if they can do it, so can we – it used to be *illegal* there even to give your children Welsh names!). Catarina was terrific, with the quite natural but unusually accented Welsh that she spoke, and the wonderful fact that she didn't speak English. This made her the first person I had ever met with whom I couldn't communicate unless I spoke Welsh, and that is an enormous spur for a learner. It is a great pity that more Welsh speakers do not simply refuse to speak English, because it would without any doubt at all result in more incomers learning Welsh.

Yes, I know that we 'all speak English anyway' (although I also know that many Welsh speakers are genuinely uncomfortable in English, because they do not speak it as well as they speak their first language, oddly enough), but that shouldn't mean we all *have* to. I'm capable of eating meat, but I'm a vegetarian, so I choose not to (well, most of the time, anyway, although I do find it hard to resist the occasional burger after a night on the town, but please don't tell my mother, who goes to a lot of trouble to have vegetarian options ready for me when I visit). Why can't we develop the language equivalent of vegetarianism? 'I choose not to speak English, because it's bad for my culture.' No, it's not usually convenient – it means waiting longer, or having to shop somewhere else, or having to risk being laughed or shouted at. But perhaps convenience shouldn't be the driving motive in our lives.

Anyway, Catarina was a real breath of fresh air for those very reasons, and it was extremely entertaining going out and around Bangor with her. We lost her in Safeways once, when we had gone to have a bite to eat at lunchtime, because she was behind us in the queue, and then just wasn't there when we were all sitting down. A few minutes later, just when we were starting to feel guilty and consider mounting a rescue party, she turned up, looking indignant.

'The girl at the counter couldn't speak Welsh!' she said, scandalised (and in Welsh, of course). 'I couldn't understand a word she was saying! I just had to put my money in my hand and let her take what she wanted!'

It was a rare pleasure to think of the confusion Catarina must have caused to the girl at the till, who just knew with the thoughtless unconcern of too many non-Welsh speakers that 'they all speak English anyway'. And it points up one of the fundamental flaws in what is meant to be a Cymru where Welsh speakers have the basic human right to use their language – practically speaking, it is often just not possible, and it won't be, until private businesses realise that they have a moral duty to make sure that all their front-line, customer-facing staff either speak Welsh or learn enough to do their job in Welsh. How long can it take to learn 'That'll be two pounds, please' in Welsh? Of course, private businesses are not exactly famous for realising that they have any kind of moral duty to anything apart from their bank balance, which is why the Assembly needs to have the political courage to require them to fulfil their moral duties, in the same way that they are required to fulfil their moral duties towards the environment. Courage doesn't seem to be the Assembly's strong suit, though. As Rhodri Morgan said once, referring to making the Assembly a full Parliament, 'We can't decide that. That's up to Westminster to decide.'

Funnily enough, that doesn't seem to have been the attitude taken by the rest of what used to be the 'British' Empire.

The other thing that really struck me about Catarina was how she used Spanish words in the middle of Welsh sentences, in exactly the same way that we do with English. It seemed so unfair – let's be honest, Spanish is a much sexier language than English, and there was something very cool about bits of it cropping up in the middle of her Welsh. I know it doesn't make much sense, because when people use too many English words in a Welsh conversation, it just seems ridiculous at best and irritating at worst, but there you go. I spent some time trying to learn the Spanish words that she used most often, but unsurprisingly I have not heard them on the streets of Porthmadog often enough since then to be able to remember them. Which means that, sadly, I've got no choice but to find the time to learn a little Spanish at some stage, and go and spend some time in Patagonia. This learning Welsh business is just grind grind grind.

I was glad that, after the initial shyness, we did develop the habit of going to the Globe for lunch – no part of any Welsh course is as important as relaxing and chatting to people in Welsh. What's more, the course itself in Bangor wasn't as effective as the Wlpan in Aberystwyth, for the simple reason that there were too many people in our class – between fifteen and twenty, instead of the eight to ten in Aber. The teachers and materials were good, but when you get less chance to talk, you inevitably get less practice, and are therefore forced to spend more time in the pub. Which is deeply unfair.

On the bright side, though, the Globe had one very pretty barmaid, but unfortunately, according to my own rules, I wasn't allowed to flirt with her. She didn't speak Welsh, that's why. I had worked out that after all the work I'd put into learning Welsh, and making sure that all my socialising was done through the medium of Welsh, I needed two more important parts to complete the jigsaw. I needed to be able to work through the medium of Welsh more often, and I needed a Welsh-speaking girlfriend. Besides, as I've said before, Welsh speakers are just more attractive, anyway.

In Bangor I first came across something that I had heard about before, but never seen – people learning Welsh because they had to for their work. Now, it strikes me as an exceptionally healthy thing that an employer should be serious enough about the language to pay for their staff to learn it, and to give them the time off work to go on intensive courses – any employer that is prepared to invest in their staff like that is admirable. However, it was clear that one or two of the people in our class didn't see it in that light themselves – they looked put-upon, bored, as if they felt the whole thing was a monstrous waste of their time. I felt sorry for them, and they didn't exactly help anyone else feel the joys of learning – maybe they need to be sold on the value of Welsh before getting sent off to courses.

As I've said before, one of the pleasures of learning Welsh is that people go to the time and trouble to arrange trips to interesting places for you, all as part of the drive to give you something to talk about, and to get you listening to people speaking Welsh. Because the fortnight in Bangor was day-time only, there wasn't as much chance for outings, but we did get taken round the Cathedral by the president of the Welsh Students' Union. It's an imposing building, even more so from the inside than on the outside, and evocative – the Church has been central to the Welsh language, and to Welsh nationalism, for almost as long as we have been a nation. And it makes you feel humble that even students, who by natural rights ought to be drinking, dancing or thinking of excuses for why they haven't written their essays, are prepared to give freely of their time simply because they respect the fact that you are trying to learn this deeply beloved language. It's unfair, really – for students, as for any other speakers of Welsh, it ought to be a background, non-political issue, that they study through Welsh because that's their language. Instead, they're forced into political agitation because it is made clear to them that the universities will never provide equally for Welsh, that if their chosen course isn't available through their first language that's just tough luck. And they get the reputation for being hostile and aggressive, and the other students (who largely speaking, with only a few honourable exceptions, can't be bothered to learn any of the language of the country in which they just happen to be doing their degree) consider them extreme single-issue fanatics.

Yet these are the very same people who will come out and tolerate and talk to unusual groups of adults (something which most students would avoid like the plague) because, once again, they are motivated by love. Most young people, in their university years, are concerned principally with themselves, with their individual hopes and dreams and problems, and don't have to worry about being told that the fate of their culture, that its very existence, lies on their shoulders. Given these kinds of pressures at this kind of age, I think it is deeply impressive how many Welsh students, instead of turning their backs on what is an obviously unequal struggle, choose to commit time and energy on a long-term, consistent basis to doing whatever they can to make a positive difference to the future of their language. It seems clear to me that they thoroughly deserve the one-site Welsh-medium university that Cymru has so pitifully yet to establish.

Almost every country in Europe has at least one university which operates entirely through the medium of the local language – but not us.

The fortnight of a non-residential course slips past even more quickly than it does when you're staying overnight, and before we'd really had a chance to grow to know each other well, it was already coming towards the end of the second week, and the same drop in numbers as you get at the end of a four-week course was starting to kick in. Once again, you make the attempt to swap phone numbers and/or email addresses, but once again you know that unless your day-to-day life brings you into contact, or that you're on a course together again at some point, the chances are not high that you will see these people again. It's an odd kind of divorce – you're all on very similar journeys towards the language, and you've got a better understanding of the shared ups and downs of those journeys than anyone apart from other Welsh learners could have, but you're going to end up out there on the seas of this wild new language on your own.

And maybe, as you get over the sadness of saying goodbye, that is a good thing after all – because each of you wants to fit in to the real heart of Cymru, not to hide away for ever in the safe company of other second-language speakers – each of you wants to become a Welsh speaker, not a Welsh learner.

Some Sex and a Hill

Some Sex and a Hill

Pennod 12 – Yn ôl i'r Cŵps

A lot of people complain about the A470, the long, slow road from the north to the south, and it's obviously not a help to the economic development of Gogledd Gorllewin Cymru. For me, though, it is a road which winds through evocative and beautiful stretches of landscape, and which is always either carrying me up to the real home that Gwynedd has become for me, up to the mountains and the forests and the places I can hide away from having to speak English, or taking me down to family and to the eighteen-mile stretch between Machynlleth and Aberystwyth that I know better than anywhere else on the face of this earth. For someone who was brought up shifting constantly from place to place, from country to country, that kind of connection matters.

So it was with a smile and a song that I packed my car with what I would need for the month, checked that I had 5p for the toll on the Cob, and let slip the clutch on my brand new Ford Mondeo. Well, brand new in my terms, anyway – a mere 90,000 miles on the clock, and in my possession for all of a couple of months. I'd had some interesting times hitching up and down the A470, including one heart-warming occasion when the train from Port was late because it had broken down somewhere near Pwllheli, and I had a temper tantrum and decided to thumb it, and very much to my own surprise actually managed to get to Machynlleth before the train, proving convincingly that it is always wise to lose your temper and go hitch-hiking randomly. But despite the interesting times, I'd also had plenty of cold, wet, miserable and stuck-by-the-side-of-the-road days, and it felt good to be in charge of deciding my own travel timetable. And yes, I do find it very hard to drive past hitch-hikers on that stretch of road now, even though most of them don't speak Welsh. That's okay, though – I just smile at them in Welsh, and turn up Radio Cymru slightly (and am then forced to pretend that I don't mind it when Radio Cymru plays songs in English, for the love of God).

I felt prepared for the course – Bangor had done the necessary work of getting me back to grips with the grammar, and I was starting to reach the point where I really was speaking Welsh more often than I was speaking English, and I had to my delight got an 'A' in the TGAU, and there was only one slight thing left to worry about. If I had to admit that I could, sort of, in an obviously not fluent but at least he's having a conversation about something other than the weather kind of way, speak Welsh... I would have to get that tattoo. Still, no need to think about that for the time being – it was at least four weeks away, and four weeks is a lifetime. If you're a particularly small, short-lived insect of some kind.

It was hard to believe that it was only a year since I had been in the same room in Penbryn, the main reception building on the Penglais campus, booking in for my first ever course. I could remember, intellectually speaking, how difficult it had been, how self-conscious and nervous (and late) I'd been, but the sheer pang of worried emotion just wasn't there any more. This time, I was walking into a situation I knew and enjoyed, looking forward to meeting another fresh set of interesting people, and looking forward perhaps most of all to renewing my acquaintance with the Cŵps. What's more, this time I was in Class 3 – no messing around with 2A or 2B, oh no. It reminded me a bit of being in my last year at school – ah, the power, the sense of seniority, the knowledge that you could give Class 1 a nervous breakdown just by *looking* at them in Welsh.

And true to form, Class 3 was a collection of fascinating people, all of whom had put real time and effort into learning Welsh, all of whom were capable of holding a sensible conversation in Welsh, and all of whom had different reasons, different emotional drivers, for carrying on to real, functional fluency. And just for once, I wasn't the only Welsh person in the class – I think it may be something to do with people who live in Cymru having more reason to keep working at it, but as you move up through the levels, you are increasingly likely to find that it is other Welsh people who are learning with you. Not that this is good or bad one way or the other, but it is a warm feeling to see other people choosing to come back to the language that should, by all rights, have been in their mouths from birth.

Our first tutor was Siwan, and we were off to a flying start. She was one of those rare teachers who are able to form a genuine bond of affection with the class at the same time as keeping a tight rein on our tendency to go off at wild tangents. She could get us to shut up and pay attention while at the same time making us feel that she would have liked to hear whatever nonsense we had to say, if only we didn't have the lesson to get on with, and that maybe later on down at the Cŵps would be a better time for us to talk at random. Needless to say, she had the class eating out of the palm of her hand within the first day, and she gave every impression that she was enjoying herself as well. The quality of teachers can make such a difference – the course itself is strong enough to make sure that you learn well even if you don't click with the teacher, but if you're lucky enough to get someone who can inspire the less certain at the same time as they challenge the more confident, it can transform the class dynamic.

The coursebook that we were working from had been given the unsettlingly imposing title of Cwrs Meistroli – meistroli, as you may already have figured out, means 'mastering', and seemed to be coming a little early in the process as far as I was concerned. Pellach was quite pell enough for me, actually, I wanted to whimper – can we leave mastering the language for, oh, say another forty years or so, please? I'm just trying to *learn* it.

But actually, by the time you're in Class 3, it's not the textbook itself so much as the attitude of the other people on the course which decides at what kind of level you're going to be learning. We were lucky – no-one in the class wanted to speak English at all at any stage, and Brieg, our resident blue-eyed Breton, insisted that he couldn't, anyway, so there was no point asking him to. I'm fairly sure he was exaggerating his lack of English, but it made for a good attitude. Brieg was a first-language Breton speaker, which fascinated me – once you start learning Welsh, you come across all sorts of other colourful Celtic peoples, and you discover that just because English language newspapers never tell you anything about them doesn't mean they don't exist, and even sometimes flourish. Brieg seemed enormously confident about the future of Breton in Brittany, and since he works as a teacher through the medium of Breton, he should know. It was also comforting that we are far from being the only minority language and culture struggling for survival against the remorseless imperialism of globalisation. It may look like an unequal struggle, but it is a crucial one, because the real truth is that the struggle now of minority cultures and languages to survive is the struggle of the entire human race to avoid ending up with no variety at all, with nothing left but a planet-wide McCulture. Anyone who wants to avoid that, whether or not they have the time and energy and commitment to learn a minority language themselves, should at the very least be supporting those who do want to learn or live through one of the smaller languages of the world.

As well as the short, stocky, sandy-coloured Brieg, on the extremist front, we also had the comparatively tall, dark Gwilym, a Welsh carpenter from London, whom I've honestly never heard utter a *word* of English. His girlfriend, Jess, was in one of the beginners' groups, but as far as I could see, Gwilym wouldn't even speak English with *her*. You've got to be slightly in awe of that kind of single-minded, determined focus. Gwilym was hoping that he was going to be able to move back to Cymru, and to live in a genuine, Welsh-speaking community – I hope he managed to, and whether he did or not, it would be wonderful to hear from him, if he happens to be reading this. Gwilym being Gwilym, though, is highly unlikely to be reading a book in English, fair play to the man. Gwilym was also the class comedian, which is an impressive achievement in a second language – he was capable of twisting almost any situation on its head with a kind of dry wit that sometimes left you feeling you ought to break out into applause.

Cwrs Meistroli actually turned out to be the best course since the original Wlpan book, mostly because the greater width of vocabulary that you've developed allows you to deal with more interesting subjects. Cwrs Pellach is, to be honest, when measured against the internationally high standards of Wlpan, a touch depressing – you learn what you need to, but the chapters all seem to be about people having serious accidents and narrowly avoiding death. Learning Welsh feels enough like a series of narrow misses as it is, so the last thing we need is reminding of the precarious nature of life on a chapter-by-chapter basis. But Meistroli comes like a howl of fresh air slamming a window open, once you've got over your sheer panic at the word meistroli itself – it's somewhere on the dividing line between language textbook and general-knowledge primer, so as well as giving you all the necessary opportunities to be practising your written and spoken Welsh, it also starts filling in the gaps in your knowledge of Welsh history and culture.

Which is another thing that staggers me – it is so easy to grow up in Cymru without ever really learning anything about the history of our country. We're more likely to learn pointless things about kings and queens of England, or the role played by Britain (in other words, England dressed up in skirts and a shield) on the world stage, than we are to find out about Rhodri Fawr or the Arglwydd Rhys, who after all did nothing more important than help shape the very country to which we belong. Without a thousand years' worth of heroic effort, the Welsh language and way of life would no more be remembered here in Cymru today than it is in Strathclyde. Yes, Strathclyde used to be part of a Welsh-speaking kingdom – that's the kind of thing that the 'British' curriculum just has no interest whatsoever in telling us about, maybe because it helps show us that we have a cultural history of which we can be genuinely proud. Welsh is not a second-class culture or a second-class language, of which we ought to be faintly ashamed because it isn't English. On the contrary, it has a longer, equally proud heritage, and if we do not know our own history, we do not know what it is that we belong to. And that word 'we' there – it's not only available to Welsh people. On the contrary – anyone who learns Welsh can choose to make themselves part of that 'we'. Cwrs Meistroli helps start to fill in the gaps in our history, and it would be fair to suggest that in doing so, it plays almost as important a role as it does in terms of helping improve the learner's grasp of the language.

Apart from the increasingly interesting content of the textbook, Siwan also had us using language in ever more ambitious ways – writing rhymes, limericks, the beginnings of poetry, all of which added bit by bit to our growing linguistic self-confidence. It was natural, by then, to spend the evening down at the Cŵps without a word of English, and the only thing missing was the company of Dafydd, Margaret and Giles. It's a little unsettling, sometimes, going back for another course in the same place – there are memories scattered all over the place, and you are reminded forcefully of the friends you had made before, and of how the friends you are making in the here and now will probably also not be with you for long beyond the end of the course. I was particularly sorry that Giles was not able to be on the course – he was still lecturing at Aberystwyth, and I was able to visit him once or twice, but he hadn't had the chance to get the time off work or to spend much time in the past year using the genuinely good level of Welsh he had acquired. It is such a pity when people acquire the language but, purely because the levels of community usage are not high enough, have to watch it slip away from them again – and this is why it is so crucial that we defend the remaining natural Welsh-speaking communities, because once we run out of them, it won't make any difference how many people in De Dwyrain Cymru try to learn the language, it just won't be properly alive any more.

One of the reasons, perhaps, that we were even more well-behaved than usual about using Welsh all the time in our evenings out was that Siwan, with the mark of the genuinely involved teacher (or, perhaps, the confirmed alcoholic), spent quite a lot of time in the Cŵps with us. It made a real difference – we were all serious enough to be using Welsh anyway, but it is a valuable bonus when you have someone on hand who can answer the occasional alcoholically blurred question about vocabulary or sentence structure. Okay, maybe you're not likely to remember the answer the next morning, but hey, it just does something for your confidence.

The first week was gone almost before it had even arrived, we were enjoying ourselves so much. When you get a group like that, an intensive course doesn't seem so much like a learning process as a continual party, where staggering bleary-eyed into class as near to nine o'clock as you can manage, and comforting yourself with coffee while you pretend you're paying attention, is just a continuation of the night out before. The first hour or so passes quickly enough, gossiping and remembering embarrassing grammatical errors in public (well, in the Cŵps, anyway, which amounts to more or less the same thing), and then hey, it's time for the coffee break, which is starting to become indistinguishable from the lessons (apart from the Penbryn coffee and occasional (oh, okay, I always ate as many as I could before people started staring) chocolate biscuit).

If it hadn't been for Siwan and her relentless ability to get us to concentrate for far more of the day than we would have believed ourselves capable, we would probably have got nowhere with the course at all. The second week was always going to be a difficult time for whoever had the thankless task of following in Siwan's footsteps – we were already asking her quite seriously not to abandon us, and her weak excuses about having a PhD to finish were frankly unacceptable. We kept thinking we were going to manage to persuade her to stay, but however much Siwan may look as though she is being swayed by your arguments, she's never really going to change her mind. We should have known – she'd never once let us get away with skipping a single exercise, after all, and it would be hard to think of a more perfect example of an iron fist concealed within a velvet glove. It was with no small amount of uncertainty, therefore, that we approached Week Two.

Some Sex and a Hill

Pennod 13 – Deffro'n Dawel

Eleri, our next tutor, was one of the most overwhelmingly detached-from-reality people I have ever met. She was genuinely lovely, full of smiles and friendliness, but every sentence in the course seemed to take her slightly by surprise, as though she'd just that minute been daydreaming about sunbathing on a beach in the Bahamas, and out of nowhere here was someone asking her a question about Welsh grammar. I almost began to feel that it was heartless of us to keep reminding her of the grim truth: she was stuck in the middle of an Wlpan class, not lounging by the side of a tropical swimming pool with a tall drink in her hand.

It was, I would have to admit, very unfair on her that she had to take us immediately after Siwan, who absolutely radiated organisation. Organisation and Eleri, one couldn't help feeling, probably went together in much the same way as teetotalism and learning Welsh. Apart from her friendliness, though, she had one other seriously winning quality to her, and that was how utterly, completely obvious it was that she lived her life through the medium of Welsh to such an extent that she clearly found it mildly puzzling that there were people who couldn't speak it. She would lapse, sometimes, into talking to us with a kind of concerned edge to her voice, as though we were slightly backwards children who really ought to be able to remember the alphabet by now, after all. Thinking about it, maybe she wasn't really that far from the truth.

But we kept on ploughing through the course, getting battered by wave after wave of new vocabulary and more complicated sentence structures, and learning layer after layer of Welsh culture and history almost by accident. Outside the class, of course, we spent most of our time heading downhill quite literally as quickly as we could – for those of you who don't know Aber, the Cŵps is at the bottom of the hill on which the University perches irreverently. The perfect mixture, really – getting to the Cŵps in the first place is easy because it's all downhill, and wading back up to Cwrt Mawr is no problem, because... er... well, because you're what we shall call 'drunk on the beauty of the Welsh language'. That, and half a dozen pints.

And we kept on being treated to arranged evening activities, which I suspect may have been Haf's way of trying to make sure that she kept us away from the

Cŵps for long enough to make sure that no-one would notice the connection between Wlpan courses and alcoholism rates. One of the best that week was a presentation from the man from Birmingham who wrote 'A Rough Guide to Wales', made all the more impressive by the fact that Mike (the Brummie in question) had been in Class 1 the year before, and was now flying on impressively through Class 3B (and was in fact to join us in 3A before the end of the course) – and he was giving the presentation in Welsh. However used to public speaking someone might be, that takes real guts. The book had made quite a stir when it came out, because some Welsh towns had objected to being called grey, miserable and boring, but if you've been to any of the towns in question (hell, no, I'm not repeating where they were, they gave Mike a hard enough time as it was), you'll know that he's a man who just tells the plain, brutal truth.

He's also the kind of person that proves beyond a shadow of a doubt that the accusations of racism against Welsh language protesters are not only vicious, bullying, dishonest and downright shameful, they are also utterly absurd. They would be laughably absurd, if only the situation was less important. Mike, you see, is a stereotypical Brummie, with an accent broad enough to park a bus on, and he's not exactly what you'd call shy and retiring. Just the kind of person the Welsh are meant to be racist towards, in fact – but Mike moved to Cymru because he fell in love with the country, and in love with the language, and the respect and affection he shows to Cymru is matched by the respect and affection every Welsh-speaking person I know who knows him feels towards him. If you're still not sure, ask Mike which he prefers – Welsh people who speak to him in Welsh, or fellow Brummies who hear his accent and come up to him and say, 'Don't blame you for moving here, mate, it's the only chance to get away from all those blacks.' It happens, I've heard him say, on a depressingly regular basis.

I know, I know – I'm repeating myself. But it's that love thing again, you see – Mike, motivated by love, is welcomed here with open arms, and is making his own valuable contribution to the future of the language. The people who think he has moved here, as they have, because there aren't as many black people in Cymru – well, whatever it is that makes them tick, it certainly isn't love.

Another key element in my acquisition of the language was happening during this second month-long visit to Aberystwyth, and it remains one of the most enjoyable things that has happened to me as a direct result of learning Welsh. I'd met Haf's husband, Joe, the year before, when he lead us around Nant yr Arian one afternoon, and spoke with enough of a Gog accent for me to find him completely unintelligible. A year later, though, and all my practice with the choir had paid off – Joe seemed to be speaking quite normally. Without really being invited, I developed the habit of dropping in without warning at their house in Bow Street, just round the corner from the sheltered housing where my Taid spent his last few years. It's a house overflowing with children and with Welsh in its most utterly natural form, so once again it was a chance for me to smile a lot and understand about 10% of what was going on. Children are a brilliant way for any experienced learner to put themselves to the test, because they will not make allowances for you. No, they'll just talk at you, and expect you to understand, and if you say something that doesn't make sense, they'll say 'Beth?!' without worrying for a second about hurting your feelings.

I found it a hugely warm place to be, and unless Haf and Joe ask me in writing to stop pestering them, I'll carry on visiting every time I'm in the area. It's like relaxing into the language equivalent of a jacuzzi, comfortable and unpredictable at the same time, with hyperactive children scattering half-formed words around randomly and over-excitedly. What's more, these days I probably understand almost half of what's going on, which is gratifying, and I've developed the unconscious habit of managing to arrive just when everyone is sitting down for a meal, which is always a bonus. In many ways, they are the family that represent for me all that is best about the warm, supportive, endlessly welcoming attitude of the Cymry to people who learn their language well enough to live through it. Which was highlighted even further when I discovered, to my very real shock, that Joe learnt the language as an adult himself – and now, if Haf isn't sure of a word, it's Joe she'll doublecheck it with. Joe's quiet air of self-assurance inspires me, and keeps me believing that I myself will have as natural, easy command of the language as he has, one day.

Meanwhile, back at the course, sometime during the second week, I became aware of what has to be the most surreal (sorry, I do of course mean the most gorwir) situation I've ever come across in the process of learning Welsh. As I hope the rest of this book shows you, that's quite a dramatic claim, but this was something that left any number of gorillas, or Scots speaking Welsh to Italians, miles behind. Not even on the same racecourse, in fact.

You'll probably think that I'm making it up (and if you do, you get full marks for realising my basic, natural dishonesty) – but just for once, I'm not. Honest. There was an incredibly old, we're talking comfortably over eighty, if not well into his second century, Japanese man roaming the campus. In fact, he was not only roaming the campus, he seemed to be attending Welsh classes. Not in Class 3, to be fair, but you'd see him sometimes with people from Class 1, and they weren't running away from him, so my guess is that he might have been in their class.

Okay, up to now you're just thinking that I'm a bit of an ageist, and that it's not that extraordinary. Perhaps not, although I've never really believed in Max Boyce's line about Welsh-speaking Japanese people. But here's the clincher, and you'll have to agree it gets weird after this – he could not speak a word of English. I mean, as in, not a word.

What?!

You see, that just leaves my brain spinning in neutral. We had an octogenarian (lowest estimate) Japanese gentleman who had crossed the world without a word of English in order to attend an Wlpan course in Aberystwyth? If you're nodding, and thinking it makes complete sense to you and why do I sound so staggered – well, I seriously think you need to have a chat with someone on a professional basis. Rumours starting going round that he was an eminent professor who had research interests in Celtic languages, and that his name was José, but how reliable can that be? I mean, since when has José been a Japanese name, for the love of tortilla? He didn't seem to speak any *Welsh*, either, so he must have been having a very peaceful time. Maybe it was a kind of bonsai thing, like those impossibly tiny, tiny trees they grow – maybe he was gathering a collection of bonsai conversations, or something like that. Even now, it still leaves me feeling blank with puzzlement, and faintly alarmed – I mean, if things like that start happening, who's to say that the floor will still be downwards the next time I take a step forward? Maybe I'd just better sit here and rest for a while, to be on the safe side. If there's anyone out there who honestly knows who he was and what he was doing, please tell me. You would be doing a kindness to one of God's less clever creatures.

At the end of the second week, I had a chance to limp back towards the most normal that my life ever gets. Yes, it was time for my second Eisteddfod, and this time, after the shock of discovering that Welsh-speaking people out in the wild (as it were) *frightened* me, I was ready for them. I knew, from my faithful attendance at the choir, that as long as I mumbled a lot and said 'Ia?' loudly at the end of each sentence, I would be doing all I needed to cover up my lack of Welsh. I was even ready for People Asking Questions (which is always the trickiest moment when you're pretending to understand what's going on – you know, when they turn to you and say 'something something very quickly something something QUESTION MARK?' and it's No Good Nodding). I had learnt to make a kind of subdued, semi-growl sort of noise in my throat, while nodding and shaking my head in a kind of random mixture. It certainly made people leave me alone, so we can chalk that one down as a success. Oh, and one other thing – I could actually talk quite a lot more *Welsh* this time round. Not enough to be over-confident, but enough to take the edge off the sheer panic that had kept hovering around in the background at Llanelli.

I'd been back in Port for the weekend, because I had a bit of work to get done, so I drove over to Dinbych on my own on the Saturday morning. Every time I drive a road I've never driven before in Cymru, it amazes me how much more of the country there is than I realise. It's something to do with maps, I think – you get used to seeing Cymru look small next to England, and tiny next to France, and you can sort of lapse into feeling that we're all pretty much within shouting distance of each other. But you get out there and start trying to walk from one side to the other, and you'll need to plan for more than a day or two. Okay, I wasn't walking, but I can see that it *would* take a long time to walk, as I drive past lazily. The high moors on the way over to Dinbych were like nothing I'd seen in Cymru before – one minute, you have enough mountains to keep you going for several millennia, the next, whoa, where did they all go? And the land seems like a series of slow waves moving towards breaking on a shore somewhere out of sight, and if you're me you can feel the lump in your throat at the thought of going to the Eisteddfod and understanding and speaking this precious language which somehow manages to be as beautiful even as the breath-taking country out of which it grew.

Now for a bit where anyone who's ever been to the Eisteddfod before is going to feel smug and superior (possibly not for the first time, since I have quite a knack for lulling other people into feeling smug and superior. Yes, of course it's deliberate). You see, it had been a fairly clear, mostly sunny sort of day in Llanelli. No. It hadn't crossed my mind that it could rain at an Eisteddfod.

Yes, har har, very funny, I know that *now* – I know *now* that rain and Eisteddfodau more or less go arm in arm (and I still haven't worked out what the point of having a Gorsedd of Druids actually is, then, if they can't even control the weather). As you'll have guessed by now, it was raining by the time I got to Dinbych, even though it had been perfectly sunny on the way over. Remember, never discount the possibility of a plot. It was obvious, even as I was parking, that getting the car out again was going to be the stuff of legend, with which I would hopefully be able to bore my grandchildren some day, and I kept getting sudden (and perfectly rational, if you ask me) urges to phone the Coast Guard. The plastic matting which had been laid down for people to walk on was bobbing around like a lilo in a swimming pool (of course I'm not exaggerating, writers never exaggerate), and reaching the main entrance felt rather like reaching shore after a particularly seasickish ferry trip. Not that it was going to get any better inside, on the Maes, of course – so I did my 'leisurely stroll round the outside of the Maes to get a feel for where everything is' in about a minute and half, hunched into the wind and the rain and hoping to God that the baked potato sellers were going to speak Welsh, since I was clearly going to have to spend the entire day in their company.

That, in fact, became the pattern of the day – a huddled refuge in the sheltered but still quite cold food park broken up by intermittent bursts of enough cultural courage to go jogging from tent to tent with the single comfort of knowing that any brief conversations I stumbled into were extremely likely to be about the weather. If you ever have to talk to an obviously nervous learner and you're not sure what to talk about, choose the weather. My *God*, we can talk about the weather.

It was on one of those excursions, knitting my way through the rows of stands, that I came across the expansive, impressive and almost entirely empty tent of the 'Welsh' Conservative Party. You wouldn't have expected me to find that of any particular interest? I don't strike you as a Tory? Well, thanks mostly to having been a student in the 1980s, I'm certainly bloody *not* – but there was a small tent tucked away next door to the lonely Tories that was a lot busier and a lot more attractive. I'd heard about Cymuned, of course, when I started reading the Welsh-language press to find out more about what had been going on with Seimon Glyn, and the more I read about them, the more I felt that this was a group of people who deserved support. The fight to stop rural communities from becoming ghostly playgrounds for the rich is a fight to protect the very fabric of society, and it's going on all over Europe. And when the death of a rural community also means the death of a language, it's a doubly important struggle. My only reservation was whether or not people who loved the language so much would be prepared to tolerate the unintentional damage I inflicted on it every time I opened my mouth – and that turned out to be the most unnecessary concern I have ever had.

I felt nervous walking into the tent, as though I was opening myself up to judgement, even though I had of course been practising several possible sentences in my mind beforehand. Learning Welsh can be quite like playing chess, sometimes – you find yourself trying to predict conversations so you can consider what phrases you could use, and which potentially tricky vocabulary attacks you need to watch out for. Unlike chess, you get it wrong about ninety-nine times out of every hundred, but I'm sure it's still good practice.

The reality, naturally, turned out to be far simpler than my projected conversations, most of which had included the weather plus some optimistic intention to say something simple, clear yet interesting about politics. Is it actually possible, it dawns on me now, to say something simple, clear and yet interesting about politics? I mean, without swearing. All I actually did was sidle in surreptitiously, grab a couple of T-shirts (because a] it's almost impossible to go into any stand in the Eisteddfod without buying a T-shirt, and b] I wanted to make it quite clear that I was more of a buyer than a talker) and then wave cheerfully in the direction of what appeared to be a membership form, saying fluently, 'Beth… sut… dwi isho… lle… ydw i…?' It's a great relief (to digress for a moment, uncharacteristically) when you finally realise that first-language speakers virtually never talk in whole, coherent sentences, and that if you do, you're actually going to sound more like a learner than if you just give in and babble vaguely. Once that struck me, I gave in and went with the flow, and have been doing very little but babbling vaguely ever since. It fits in particularly naturally in the Cŵps.

Nobody, it became immediately clear, was going to refuse to take my membership money on the grounds that my Welsh wasn't good enough. I wasn't even asked to take some kind of on-the-spot grammar and pronunciation test, fair play to Cymuned. I walked out back into the rain a changed person, having made my first ever political gesture, shining like a good deed in a naughty world – none of which, unfortunately, stopped me from feeling cold and wet, but hey, says the voice of experience, that's the National Eisteddfod for you. What I had no way of knowing at that stage was how crucial those five minutes were going to be in my personal process of acquiring the Welsh language as a natural medium of conversation – it was Cymuned, or to be precise the local groups in Eifionydd and Penrhyndeudraeth, that would offer me the context within which I could become a Welsh speaker. I have never, not on a single occasion, been made to feel unwelcome as a learner in any meeting, assembly or rally, I have never been treated impatiently when I have struggled to express myself clearly, I have never been given anything other than the warmest encouragement and support. Why should members of pressure groups, without really even thinking about it, provide such an immaculately perfect environment for Welsh language learners? It's simple – you're learning and using the language they love.

As you can probably tell, I had reached the point in my journey towards the language where I could see how *difficult* it was to live entirely through the medium of Welsh even if I was confident enough to try. I had realised, in other words, that there was a very real risk that I had come back to the language just in time to witness it slipping away for good, which is an intolerable thought – like falling in love, and then finding out that the person you love is dying.

The language will not die, though; this will not be allowed to happen – because it is simply not an acceptable option. If you agree about that, go and join something *now* – Plaid Cymru, Cymdeithas yr Iaith, Merched y Wawr – any group of people who are trying to keep the language alive. I'll wait here until you've found one and signed up.

No, it's not a rhetorical device, I *meant* it. Go on, off with you. It'll only take two minutes, and then I'll stop badgering you about it.

Yes, I *promise*.

Some Sex and a Hill

Pennod 14 – Meddwi ar Iaith

After such an emotional weekend, it felt more than a little odd to be back in Aberystwyth, where the world hadn't changed, where no-one was marching on the council buildings or tearing down the infrastructure of oppression. For a while, I'd felt carried away to such an extent that I had rather conveniently forgotten that I still had a very great deal of work to do if I was to learn the language in the first place.

Fortunately, we had just the right tutor to get me firmly back on track. At short notice, Rob had agreed to take our class, and since a few people in both 3A and 3B had only been able to get the first fortnight off work, what remained of the two groups were being brought together. It's quite a challenge to blend two groups after they have already been on the course for a fortnight – you've got two clear, different class dynamics, and two clear, different group identities. It all went better than I had secretly expected, because 3B were a friendly group and, in Mike's case in particular, had a lot to offer in class discussion – but you could see the understated traces of 'them' and 'us' right through to the end of the month.

Rob is a full-time Welsh tutor, and the difference showed. It was clear, for example, that he was at no stage daydreaming about lounging by the side of a tropical swimming pool with a tall drink in his hand while legions of admirers gazed longingly at his not exactly luxuriantly curly waves of short brown hair. He'd hammered Welsh into skulls every bit as thick as ours for years, and apart from the occasional wince when people looked as though they wanted him to explain how and when 'yn' causes a soft mutation, you could tell he was on familiar, comfortable territory. Welsh classes are a bit like horses – if a teacher is at all uncertain or disorganised, we get skittery and prone to panic, but a firm hand on the reins helps us calm down and concentrate. What's more, Rob seemed to have a slightly different attitude to Class 3 than I remember from Class 2B the year before – that is, not a word of English, which suited us. I think Rob is probably prone to the same kind of despair that Giles had begun to feel in Class 2B after a fortnight's conversation about the weather and learning Welsh – the feeling that you might not have much longer to live if you don't get to talk about something interesting soon. The conversation in Class 3, it seemed, had just about managed to get to the point where Rob could ward off despair for several hours in a row before sneaking out for the equivalent of a quick smoke in the shape of a chat with another tutor.

And please don't get the wrong impression – we were working very hard by this stage. Someone, somewhere (and I blame Haf, of course) appeared to have decided that we ought to try and finish the Cwrs Meistroli, and we were rattling through it at a giddying pace. If we had been horses, and had panicked and bolted, we just couldn't have gone much faster anyway. With hindsight, I think it was probably a good thing, although it felt quite intense at the time – when you're struggling just to keep up, and you're getting paragraph after quick test after paragraph thrown at you endlessly, you start to get brief flashbacks (or perhaps flashforwardses) where you reach what is, after all, the ultimate aim: you understand increasingly large chunks of Welsh without having to translate it into English. You have to – you don't have enough time to translate, or you'll be late for your coffee break.

At this stage in the process of learning Welsh, coffee breaks have changed from being eerily quiet ceremonies where the hush is broken only by the occasional brave soul venturing a quick 'O ble dych chi'n dod?' into something much more like a proper coffee break – gossip, biscuits, coffee and gossip. They are, if you like, the day-time version of the Cŵps Although it *is* important to do the leg-work of learning grammar and vocabulary, it's in the Cŵps or the coffee break that you are starting to take real, significant steps towards using the language. There's an enormous difference between understanding a language and actually using it, and you can work from books for your entire life without actually being able to speak a language if you don't get out there and practise *speaking*.

By the third week, too, some of the learners in 2A were starting to show signs of willingness to have conversations with us, with us the masters of the Wlpan universe. Frankly, I thought it was quite cheeky of them – when I was in Class 2, I wouldn't have dreamed of having the nerve to start chatting to one of the near-fluent god-like figures in Class 3. Perhaps we weren't doing quite as good a job of appearing near-fluent and god-like. Becky and Karen were the two most talkative – they were students who had been taking weekly classes for a while at the university, and had clearly paid a lot more attention to the language than is true of the vast majority of non-Welsh students. Becky was from England, and Karen from Germany, and both of them sounded as though they would much rather stay in Cymru than anywhere else – an attitude which makes a lot of sense to me. Becky seemed to wave her arms around quite a lot when speaking or listening to Welsh, as though she wanted to pretend that she was drowning, while Karen had the permanent look of concentration that comes from someone who has been made to take too many exams. They both spoke much better Welsh than they seemed to realise, which I suspect may be true of all learners (apart from me).

Robin Huw Bowen came to play harp for us again that week, underlining what I have already said about the commitment of people who are prepared to go to all sorts of lengths to support those of us who make the effort to learn Welsh. Apparently bored and wanting to liven things up, Haf decided to announce cheerfully that I would introduce the eminent harpist. In Welsh.

Remember what I said earlier about Mike? About how even if you're *used* to speaking in public, doing it in a language you're busy trying to learn is a bit of a shark-filled proposition? Well put it this way, I was *not* used to talking in public. I can't remember a single one of the words that tumbled in a random, haphazard mess out of my mouth, but I can remember that when I sat down again afterwards, Swyn, one of Haf's several hundred daughters, was doing her best to pretend that she wasn't sniggering. She'll deny this, of course. She claimed the other day that she now feels self-conscious about her own use of mutations when I'm around, on the fairly weak grounds that I have done so much work on mutations that I'll be able to tell when she gets them wrong. The innocent naïvety of youth. Sadly, that's the kind of (albeit back-handed) compliment that most learners are physically incapable of believing.

We also had a sing-along session one evening that week which Haf, with great insight into our group dynamic, had arranged in the Cŵps. This time, diolch i'r drefn, there was nothing that needed introducing, and I got to blend in with the background a bit more successfully. The outgoing, piano-playing Jamie Medhurst, another man who gives generously of his time to help tempt learners down the straight and narrow path of Welsh-speaking revelry, was very much in charge of the evening – all the rest of us had to do was follow the songsheets we were given. Of course, I did have one slight advantage over the rest of the group – six months of singing with the choir meant that various patterns of 'Fwd-la-la' held no fear for me. Fwd-la-la, di-la-la-laaa… sorry, that's me showing off, just because I can.

It must be quite a gorwir experience for normal Welsh speakers who happen to find themselves in the Cŵps when a crew of learners takes over the place and starts singing, with wild and often inaccurate enthusiasm, all the most predictable songs you could imagine – 'Cyfri'r Geifr', 'Moliannwn', 'Milgi Milgi',

'Ar Lan y Môr', you name it. I know that if the same thing were to happen tonight, when I plan on popping into the Cŵps for a quick pint, I would probably have to run away in sheer self-defence. Mind you, the exuberance of it all must be quite an entertaining spectacle, and it's very comfortable for the learners – we're sitting there with a sheet of ready-made, pre-prepared words and sentences in front of us, after all. Try and engage us in a conversation, and you're quite likely to get 'Oes gafr eto?' or 'Fe awn am dro i'r dref' thrown back at you. Or, if you're particularly lucky, we might just say 'Rwy'n dy garu di' at you over and over, because we really have learnt that sentence by now. We almost definitely don't actually *mean* it, though, so don't get carried away.

It might have been after the sing-along night in the Cŵps that I had one of my more memorable and encouraging experiences (no, very sorry, this isn't going to be where I talk about sex). After the Cŵps, we'd gone on somewhere else, and it was quite late by the time Melissa, Judith, Brieg and I staggered towards the taxi rank, having decided that for once, the idea of the hill being nice and easy when you've had enough to drink wasn't sufficiently convincing. I ended up in the front seat, and the taxi driver didn't speak Welsh, so I was the mug who got saddled with having to talk in English for the first time that evening (and I don't care what your first language is, starting to swap between languages at that time of night is asking for trouble – that taxi driver is quite lucky I didn't end up speaking broken Italian to her).

Yes, I know, nothing very memorable there yet. We got safely up the hill, tumbled out of the cab by Cwrt Mawr, and weaved our individual paths back towards our own rooms (I did warn you there wasn't going to be any sex in this bit). And it was lying there in my bed, hiccuping my way to sleep, that it dawned on me belatedly that I had been talking Welsh to the drunken rabble in the back of the cab, and English to the taxi driver, without even thinking about it. Speaking English to Brieg and the others hadn't even crossed my mind – I hadn't had to make any special effort to talk Welsh to them, I just quite simply could no longer even imagine not.

Okay, that doesn't look quite as thrilling written down as it did when I realised it, flat on my back and riding to sleep with the horses in the high fields, but believe me it was a watershed moment. A learner spends so much time having to concentrate, having to think about words and phrases and sentence structures and vocabulary, that when they realise they have been talking Welsh without being consciously *aware* of it, for the first time, it is an intoxicating feeling. Even if they're already drunk. This, after all, is what I have been working towards – I don't want to spend my life speaking Welsh by keeping a little poster stuck up in the back of my mind with 'Defnyddiwch y Gymraeg' written on it in bold black letters, I want to speak Welsh because that is the natural thing to do. There was a broad smile on my face that night, and I slept the sleep of the blessed, because however briefly, however drunkenly, I had just taken my first step into life as a 'real' Welsh speaker.

Some Welsh learners become disheartened at the length of the journey towards the language, and some fall by the side of the road and make their own compromises with the world in English, but for me one of the lasting joys of this new tongue in my mouth is the never-ending number of first steps I find myself taking. Every time I do something in Welsh that I've never done before, it raises the hairs on the back of my neck – first steps, after all, are so much more interesting than any other. In fact, it doesn't even need to be a first step for me – although this might sound hard to fathom to a natural first-language Welsh speaker, every single sentence I manage to say in Welsh fills my heart with a sense of privilege. Every single conversation I have through the medium of Welsh wraps a warm, honey-textured layer of pure, uncompromising happiness around me. It's hard work getting there, but yes, it's worth it.

It was inevitable, really, with all the love and politics swimming around inside my increasingly addled, vocabulary-burdened mind, that I should carry on joining protest groups. That was the week I took my courage in both hands again, and went off to find the office of Cymdeithas yr Iaith (the Welsh Language Society). It was a very different thing to joining Cymuned, for me – I'd heard precious little about the Cymdeithas since I'd been back in Cymru, but as long as I could remember I'd known that I would be a member 'one day', in the semi-mythical time that would come when I spoke Welsh. However absurd it may seem, the Tafod y Ddraig and the words 'Deddf Iaith Newydd' have been chalked on blackboards, doodled on exam papers, inked on ring-files and sometimes just drawn in the mist of my breath on airplane windows across the whole wide planet. I may not have known much about them, but I knew one thing – they stood for being Welsh, they stood for arwahanrwydd and perhaps, in a world where everyone tried to persuade me I came from England, they stood very simply and clearly for not being English.

One of the standard, lazy attacks on Welsh nationalists that I find most straightforwardly unintelligent is this old chestnut about how pathetic it is that Welsh nationalism defines itself by not being English, by opposition to England. Apart from the fact that it's an absurdly sweeping statement, and completely ignores huge swathes of cultural celebration, it's just so obviously inevitable. Against all the odds, we have somehow maintained our nationality and separate identity while tucked uncomfortably into the very midriff of what was for a long time the most powerful nation on earth, home of what has become the world's common language, which has for centuries done everything within its power to turn Cymru into England. Pointing out that despite everything, we are still not England is just another way of celebrating what we are. If they hadn't been trying so hard to make us into England, we wouldn't be so proud of the fact that they've failed.

To my slight disappointment, there were no fanfares of trumpets when I walked into the Cymdeithas office. They just gave me a form to fill in, and took my money. I mean, no-one even *clapped*. They seemed to think it was normal that I spoke Welsh, and I had to control the urge to inflict the whole, thirty year story on them, and to tell them about the Tafod y Ddraig in the corner of my blackboards in Zimbabwe and Dubai, and explain why it was that I was going to have to dance around the office for a while, and ask them politely if they would mind ululating while I did so. They didn't really look in the mood to ululate, though, so I just carried on pretending that I was normal, instead. And being normal in Welsh is such a staggeringly unusual thing for me that it made up for not having a victory dance.

Well, not having a victory dance until I got back to my flat in Cwrt Mawr, actually, but how I choose to make a fool of myself in private is my own business. Go on, off with you – you go and read the next chapter, and leave me here waving my arms, stamping my feet and ululating. I really *love* that word.

Some Sex and a Hill

Some Sex and a Hill

Pennod 15 – Draig Waedlyd

As I've said before, the last week of an intensive Welsh course is always a time of mixed emotions, but on this occasion we had one piece of heartlifting news – Siwan was coming back to teach us again. This gave us a fresh impetus just at a time when otherwise we would have been sinking into the quiet introspection that can strike you at the end of the course. There was a general feeling that we wanted to show Siwan that we had actually got *better*, that we hadn't given up once she wasn't there to organise us any more, and then there was just the pleasure of seeing her again. Siwan, you see, quite clearly thought of us as 'her' group, and in my experience classes of any age respond with strange but real enthusiasm to teachers who are in any way possessive of them.

I know that worked for me, anyway – when I taught in Dubai, I was fiercely possessive of my form group for five long years, and considered it almost rude when they went to other classes. The one year they spent being taught English by someone other than me was appalling, although on the bright side it was obviously appalling to them as well. They genuinely disliked their new teacher, which was partly why I got them back again the next year. Did I, like a true professional, try and persuade them to see the good points in the thief who had stolen them from me for that year? I'll leave you to work that out for yourself. But the moral is that they could see I felt possessive about them, and long years down the road I still get regular emails from several of them. Affection breeds affection, more often than not.

And that was why we were so glad to see Siwan again, even though it also meant we had the unexpected shock of being expected to *work* again.

'Does neb yn gweithio yn 'rwythnos olaf!' – we did our best to persuade her, but it was obvious that we were fighting a losing battle. She'd smile, listen to what we wanted to say, and then start handing out exercises and getting the tape recorder ready, and before we'd even had a real chance to finish moaning, we'd find ourselves in the middle of a piece of *work*. By this stage, all the other classes were doing nothing apart from working on their sketches for the Prynhawn Llawen on the Thursday of that week, but Siwan wouldn't even let us take much time off for that – an hour here or there, if we were lucky and behaved ourselves properly, and the rest of the time we were going to work flat out because that's what we were there for. It's almost impossible to argue with someone who can order you around that bluntly without stopping smiling.

The sketch was on all our minds. We were lucky, because we had Mike in our class now, and it's always handy having a professional entertainer and comedian in your corner when it comes to preparing for a Prynhawn Llawen. What's more, Mike and I both remembered not being able to understand a word from the Class 3 sketch the year before, so we were determined to keep everything we did as simple as possible, which strikes me as a pretty good rule of thumb in any kind of 'just write something funny now' kind of situation.

Actually, I say that the sketch was on all our minds, and it was true, but it wasn't on my mind as much as on everyone else's. No, I had something else that was nagging away at me, and about which I was in fact considerably more nervous than I was about the sketch, which itself shows that I really was a lot more comfortable in Welsh by then than I had been the year before. And that was the problem, you see – it really did feel as though I could speak Welsh well enough to get by. In other words, as though you could, if you were charitable, describe me as having a certain fluency in the language.

And that meant it was time for my tattoo.

When I was younger, I had a phobia about needles. I used to get quite animated when trying to explain to my mother that I would much rather catch yellow fever or whatever was available in the new country to which we were moving than have the injection. It seemed quite simple to me – certain pain and misery with the injection, or just a possible tropical disease which couldn't be as bad as the injection anyway. Disappointingly, my mother never seemed to understand my carefully prepared lines of argument. Only twice did I ever have an injection that didn't cause me pain and misery. The first was in the surgery in Borth, when the perceptive doctor said,

'You look worried. Do you feel like screaming?'
Naturally, I nodded fiercely.
'Well go on then,' he encouraged me, 'scream.'

So I did. Very enthusiastically. And just as I finished, he injected me, and I was too tired to notice. I'd call it the perfect solution, if it hadn't been for the real fear I saw on the faces of the patients in the waiting room on our way out – several of them looked as though they were giving serious consideration to finding a surgery where innocent young children such as myself were not brutally tortured in broad daylight. The other time was when an apparently nice nurse told me to roll up my left sleeve, and to relax my arm. While she was swabbing the bulgingly tense veins on my bare upper left arm, the doctor injected me quickly in my right. Sneaky, but you have to hand to it them – effective.

That's me and needles. I couldn't even watch injections on TV, and usually had to leave the room when the mother and brother insisted on watching 'Casualty'. I still have a faint suspicion that they only *pretended* to be watching 'Casualty' until they succeeded in driving me out, and then promptly switched channels, but that's a paranoid story for a different day. And here I was, giving serious, real consideration to having a bloody great Draig Goch tattooed on me. I wish I could blame someone else, but no, it was definitely all my own stupid idea.

And this time, there was no way out. In the first week, remembering how I'd backed out the year before, I'd made sure that I told everyone what I was planning to do, so that the sheer weight of peer expectation would force me to go through with it. If I'd been able to go back in time at the beginning of the fourth week, I would have given myself a really good kicking for being such a manipulative git.

Some Sex and a Hill

The tattoo shop at the foot of Penglais Hill is where I went, browsing through the different dragon designs while pretending that I wasn't feeling sick to the stomach. In the end, I settled for a clean, traditional dragon (without, needless to say, the white and green background, which really would have been a bit more pain than was strictly necessary, thank you), and the next thing I knew I was leaning forward, holding on to the side of the victim chair, and having my left shoulder blade swabbed. It crossed my mind briefly that it might be a bluff, and that they were going to tattoo me on my right shoulder, but tattooists appear not to think that imaginatively. Besides, a tattoo takes a damned sight longer, as I can now vouch.

It doesn't really hurt to begin with – you just feel as though you've caught a smallish splinter, something like that. For a moment, you feel relieved – this tattooing business, you decide, is no problem, a piece of cake, nothing to worry about. What was all that nonsense about letting them know if you thought you were going to faint or throw up? Ha! Then, it carries on. And it carries on carrying on. And it carries on carrying on for quite a while, and meanwhile they have apparently put the central heating up because you are beginning to sweat, and you didn't realise that the room was so small or that you were sitting at such a peculiar, dizzyness-inspiring angle. And it carries on carrying on, and you understand all of a sudden that you are in something akin to Purgatory, and that you would take enormous, extreme, and possibly even unfair pleasure out of throwing up over the tattooist's shoes. But despite their warnings, there's a mad little caveman voice inside you shouting that it would be pathetic and childish to beg him to stop and let you lie down for a while and perhaps cry a bit. So you keep your mouth shut, and sway a little from time to time, and think about things that have got nothing at all to do with vomit.

When he stops for a moment, and asks if you're feeling okay, you manage to nod faintly.

'Glass of water and a bit of a rest?' he asks, and you nod again, in an 'Oh, yeah, sure, why not, if *you* need a breather' sort of way, while making a mental note to add him to your list of souls to pray for. But then, after you've succeeded in keeping the water down, he wrecks it all by starting again, and this time you're already fairly sore, so yes, it hurts from the very beginning, and you watch the way the colours on the wall are all moving back and fro like a ship at anchor.

When it's finally all over, the caveman inside you leaps around beating his chest, and you say thank you in an offhand a voice as possible, as if, hey, you've suffered worse things than that in the jungles of Malaysia. All you've *actually* suffered in the jungles of Malaysia is the occasional hunger pang, which doesn't really compare, but he doesn't need to know that.

And that's it. Simple. I'd do it again at the drop of a hat, no problems. Which is why I have NO other tattoos. I walked back up the hill feeling a bit short on blood, but long on self-satisfaction, and the not entirely rational feeling that I had suffered pain on behalf of being Welsh. As martyrdom goes, I'll admit it's not *that* impressive, but they didn't offer burning at the stake in that particular tattooist. Of course, I had to concentrate not to pick at it for quite a while, as the scabs formed, but on the bright side, everyone wanted to see it, and it was a remarkably neat piece of work. I've never had to take my shirt off on such a regular basis in public – and I'm sorry, but that's about as sexy as this chapter is going to get. These days, I quite often forget it's there, but whenever I do happen to remember, I'm quietly glad that I had it done. It may not be original, it may not be important in the broad scheme of things, but it's another quiet, clear statement about where my heart lies. It was in the Canolfan y Celfyddydau, by the way, when Haf asked if it was true about the tattoo, and when I showed her it was, promptly screamed. For a nasty moment, I thought maybe there was a tarantula on my back (I've always hated that bit in Indiana Jones), but it seems that Haf just thought it was funny enough to scream. Don't ask me – perhaps it's what they call feminine logic.

Once I'd got over the thrill of the tattoo, I could start fretting about the sketch again. I don't know if they still do them now that they've been stupid enough to lose Haf as the intensive course organiser, but Prynhawniau Llawen are the perfect way to finish a course. Everyone lets their hair down and loses a lot of their usual linguistic inhibitions, and the party atmosphere is noticeably celebratory. As it ought to be – this is fifty or more people, after all, who have just put in four weeks of almost non-stop hard work and drinking, and who have almost without exception all got significantly better at speaking and understanding Welsh. That is without a doubt something worth celebrating.

The sketches themselves don't tend to stay in the memory, but I do recall Class 2A being a train that increased speed with different sentences from the Wlpan course instead of the more traditional chugging sounds; 'Mae… hi'n… oer, mae… hi'n… oer, beth.. ydy'ch.. enw.. chi, beth.. ydy'ch.. enw.. chi, o ble dych chi'n dod, o ble dych chi'n dod…' You can hear it getting faster, can't you? Well, it worked for me, or maybe it was just the way they all made sort of wheel motions with their arms. And I can remember Mike in full Lily Savage mode, and Gwilym opening the proceedings in a white druidic robe with what could only be described as a downright droopy tinfoil sword, in a perfect match for his air of deeply solemn ceremony. And, of course, the sketch I was in, in which a learner had to translate between a Gog and a Hwntw – no, not very original, I'll grant you that, but at least we seemed to have kept it simple enough for everyone to either enjoy or pity, depending on their mood.

And that was it – the end of another course. This time, there seemed to be a better chance that some of us would keep in touch; I had swapped quite a few email addresses, and have heard a fair bit since then from Brieg, Judith and Siwan. I'm still promising Brieg that I'm going to learn Breton and visit him for a change, instead of expecting him to come over to Cymru every summer – I've bought the books, Brieg, I'm working on it. I'll get there in the end, honest.

Two August courses.

That was all it had taken to get me to the stage where I felt comfortable at the prospect of living my life entirely through the medium of Welsh.

As I've said before, this is about the sheer quality of Welsh-language adult education – don't tell yourself that I must be some kind of natural language learner, and it would never work for you, because *nothing* could be further from the truth. Remember, I've struggled and failed with other languages again and again, even when I've worked at them for years – but here in Cymru, we have a system that matches the best in the world. If you'd like to get the language but you think you wouldn't be able to, commit to two intensive August courses in a row, take them seriously (as described in the rest of this book, so you'll need lots of beer and pizzas) and you'll discover that you too can be bilingual.

Some Sex and a Hill

Pennod 16 – Popeth yn Gymraeg

Once you have enough of the language to live from day to day without English, it is not an overstatement to say that your world changes.

Oh, it *looks* the same – the sky is still blue, grey or black, the fields and mountains run the range of greens and browns, the air has the same fresh morning taste to it if you manage to get up early enough – but everything has changed. You're attuned to a completely different subset of life, and you know what is going on in Cymru as well as in Wales, these two different countries that sit overlapping each other so closely and often so uncomfortably. You can read Welsh-language newspapers, you can listen to Welsh-language radio, and you hear about the things about which the English-language newspapers would never bother troubling you, because of this insanely widely accepted falsity that non-Welsh speakers couldn't possibly be interested in anything to do with the language or culture of Cymru.

And, of course, learning Welsh is something that you never stop. You just move on to different levels, and learn in different, more natural ways. I can't do any more four-week intensive courses now, I have had to realise (with a dose of disappointment) – I wouldn't fit in any more, which means the courses have succeeded. Their aim, after all, is to send you beyond the classroom and out into the world – I am improving my Welsh now in pubs and at work and every time I talk to my friends. I never sit down with vocabulary lists any more – if a word I don't understand comes up often enough, at some point I discover that I sort of understand it from the different contexts in which I have heard it, and just occasionally I'll need to check it in a dictionary. Natural linguistic growth, the kind you see in children. It's a good place to be.

And, of course, I keep on taking first steps. One of the most important so far was in the January after I got my tattoo, when I had started working as a technical writer with an environmental consultancy in Bangor. My first piece of work with them was to prepare a tender for a feasibility study looking at the possible locations for a Canolfan Adar in memory of the extremely popular Welsh naturalist and photographer Ted Breeze Jones. When we won the contract, it was clear that a significant part of the decision had been because we had committed to working through the medium of Welsh, and it was with a sense of shock that I realised that the company expected me to be one of the two main points of contact for the Gweithgor.

The first project meeting was one of the more unnerving experiences of my life. I felt like a complete fraud, and I had serious reservations about the moral stance of offering a very new Welsh learner as the point of contact for a group who wanted to work in Welsh. I was, not surprisingly, extremely quiet, and spent a lot of the meeting nodding, and fighting off strong urges to stand up and apologise dramatically for being nothing more than a second-rate, pretend Welsh speaker. Fortunately for company turnover, though, I couldn't – I was too nervous to figure out how to say it in Welsh.

Besides, nobody was actually shouting at me for being a fake, and when towards the end of the meeting I was cornered into having to say something, not a single person laughed mockingly, which I found encouraging. Over the next two months, as the Gweithgor realised that I was an enthusiastic if incomplete learner, I was shown enormous and consistent kindness. If I stumbled while expressing myself, no-one started drumming their fingers; if I mispronounced words, no-one ever hit me – where, I wanted to ask sometimes, was the famous intolerance of the Cymry Cymraeg towards learners? It just doesn't exist, as I was learning. Oh, of course you'll get the odd comment, if you make a real mess of a sentence in a crowded pub – but if you're serious about learning this language, you will be treated with respect and even admiration (quite often more than you *deserve*, if you're like me, but chalk that up as a perk of the trade).

After the project meetings, a few members of the Gweithgor would almost always go for a quiet drink, and I was invited every time. At first, I thought they were just being polite, but gradually it became clear that these people were becoming real friends of mine, and the chance to carry on talking about the Canolfan in more relaxed circumstances was doing great things for my command of the necessary vocabulary. Test me now, and I can rattle on about astudiaethau dichonoldeb and goblygiadau ariannol until you're blue in the face (which sometimes doesn't take very long, admittedly, but I find it interesting, and that's the main point as far as I am selfishly concerned). Sometimes, in the middle of an intense discussion about the possibility of boat trips across the Glaslyn estuary as part of the Canolfan 'package', or some other point of detail, I would find myself briefly amazed that after thirty years of living with the loss of the language like a constant sore, I was all of a sudden engaged in professional matters in the medium of Welsh. The process of learning, at times like that, would seem telescoped down into a simple decision, and I would forget the hours and hours of classroom work, and just feel a clear, water-coloured body-filling gratitude that I had stood up and decided that I wanted my language back.

Several members of the Gweithgor were, almost inevitably, also members of Cymuned, which accelerated my growing sense of belonging. By this stage, the other deeply significant impact on my improving Welsh was the local branch of Cymuned that met in Chwilog – Cangen Eifionydd. Here, you'd think, if anywhere, I would manage to find extremists who would mock my limited grasp of the language, and show obvious scorn for the fact that I considered myself Welsh – but here, instead, I found the most passionate and supportive Cymry Cymraeg any learner could hope to meet. It was, like a sinister, grown-up version of our classroom games, a thoroughly 'gorwir' experience reading the vicious attacks on Cymuned in the English-language press for being racist and inward-looking and negative and all the rest of that rubbish, that deeply immoral and lazy journalism, while I was getting to know a group of people who were motivated by love, who were celebratory and determined and positive and endlessly, endlessly open and encouraging towards learners.

Not once, not on a single occasion, did anyone in Cymuned ever respond to the fact that I am a learner with anything other than pleasure at the fact that I have come back to the language. In fact, if anything they tend to celebrate it rather too much, to the extent of frequently introducing me to people as 'Aran – mae o 'di dysgu Cymraeg, 'sti!' – which is all very kind of them, but tramples over the fact that I still have that deeply ingrained learner's desire to draw as little attention as *possible* to the fact that I'm a second-language Welsh speaker. The stereotypes are the wrong way round, in fact – for Welsh speakers, the fact that I've learned the language is a straightforward, positive thing. It is for me that it remains a complicated subject, because I would still give the world to have grown up through the medium of Welsh, to have that natural first-language easiness of usage that is still, as yet, only available to me in English. Yes, I'm proud of having reached the stage where I speak Welsh more often than English, but something inside me remains angry that, thanks to the deliberate undermining of our language by five hundred years of English rule, I was forever robbed of Welsh as my mother tongue. It is a theft that cannot be paid for, a blatant and brutal attempt to disembowel me of my nationality, and the reason that, like hundreds if not thousands of other people, I will spend the rest of my life doing what I can to fight for Cymru Rydd and a flourishing language is a very simple one – I do not want anyone else to have to suffer this same loss.

So, in a properly Celtic pattern of numbers, three separate things were driving me towards greater fluency – my work with the Gweithgor, my involvement with Cymuned, and my membership of the choir. Each was helping weave a life for me which happened straightforwardly and naturally through the medium of Welsh, and it would almost have been easy for me to stop even thinking about learning Welsh, and to lapse onto a permanent auto-pilot. But I knew that there was one fairly serious gap in my command of the language, and that was writing. I hadn't read many Welsh books, I'd written virtually nothing outside of various classes – I was a functional illiterate in my much-loved second language, and that was an embarrassment. Only one thing for it, then – I needed something formal to focus on, and the obvious choice was 'Defnyddio'r Gymraeg Uwch', which is effectively the A Level for Welsh as a Second Language.

The knowledge that I had an exam coming up, coupled with the purely practical need to complete my various projects (which boiled down to 'write about lots of different things in Welsh' and 'record yourself on tape talking about lots of different things in Welsh') did the necessary trick, and got me working conscientiously again, albeit mostly on my own. I signed up for another 'Sgwrs a Stori' class in Bangor, intending to go for two hours once a week on work time, but then we always seemed to be too close to one deadline or another in the office, and I didn't manage to turn up very often at all. I'd been given lots of practice materials by the Addysg Barhaus people in Bangor, though, and I worked quite hard at those – true to type, once it had really sunk in that I was sitting the A Level, I became mildly psychotic about wanting to do as well as possible. In other words, either an 'A' or lifetime exile in a monastery in Tibet was how I was seeing it.

The trickiest thing, as pretty much anyone who sits the TGAU or the Lefel A will tell you, is getting the Cymry Cymraeg to agree under *any* circumstances to let you record a five-minute talk with them.

'O na,' they'll say absurdly, 'dydy 'Nghymraeg i ddim yn ddigon da, mi wyt ti'n siarad Cymraeg yn well na fi.' Oh right, you want to snarl at them, that why you're first-language fluent and I'm struggling to understand people any time the background noise gets above 'silent'. I was aware, at this point, that Richard Brunstrom, then Chief Constable of North Wales Police, was also going to be sitting his Lefel A that summer, and I had a jealous suspicion that he could probably just *order* people to let him record a five-minute conversation with them. It may not have helped much that I didn't have a tape recorder, either. In the end, I managed to lure Rhys from work (who to my huge surprise and admiration was the drummer with such a faultless sense of timing that he left Anhrefn before they became famous) into the fifteen-minute talk about 'My use of Welsh in the workplace' by offering him a pint and smuggling a tape recorder into the pub before he realised what I was doing, and not long afterwards scooped all three of my 'Five-minute general conversations' by cornering a group of Cymuned members in the pub after a heart-warmingly successful and sunny rally in Pwllheli. Sy'n atgoffa fi – diolch o galon i'r tri ohonoch, oeddech chi wirioneddol yn garedig iawn i helpu allan fel'na.

All would have been well if only I hadn't made the appalling mistake of listening to the tape before I sent it in.

If you're studying for any exam in Welsh, and you have to record yourself, do NOT under ANY circumstances for WHATEVER reason listen to the tape before you send it in. I went from being a fairly relaxed, increasingly confident user of the language to a shattered, broken wreck in the space of about ten minutes, and it was a good month before I had the nerve to open my mouth in Welsh again. I sounded so *stupid!* I had no idea – all this time, I'd been sounding like some kind of hydrogen-breathing donkey in the middle of a nasty operation, and people had just treated me *normally*. Listening to that tape made me give very serious consideration to the possibility of becoming a Welsh-medium Trappist monk, and even today I still do everything I can to listen to anything and everything apart from myself when I'm talking Welsh.

Still, at least it's a good excuse for talking complete tripe. 'Oh, I'm sorry, didn't that make any sense at all? I never listen to myself, you see, not since I realised what I sound like. No, no, of *course* you don't have to either.'

The written exam itself, held in the familiar surroundings of Plas Tan y Bwlch where I had spent so much time in meetings with the Gweithgor Canolfan Adar Ted Breeze Jones, was a cakewalk by comparison, made awkward only by the fact that several of the other examinees were talking English to each other. As I've said before, that's sheer *madness* – once again, I'd quarantined myself from English speakers for a week before the exam, and there I was being ambushed by them just when I should have been at my most absolutely safe. Please, if you're going to sit an exam in Welsh, if you're going to do courses in Welsh, wake up to the fact that talking English slows down the learning process. Keep English out of the classroom, and for the love of all that's holy do NOT speak English at all on the day of your exam. Just say 'no'. Well, don't actually say 'no', obviously, because that would be speaking English, but I'm sure you know what I *mean*.

Fortunately for me, the examination board were clearly well practised in deciphering random brays and squeals, and they also didn't mind the fact that all my conversations had been recorded in pubs, because when the results dropped through my letterbox shortly before the National Eisteddfod in Tyddewi, there was the 'A' I'd needed if I was going to allow myself to carry on living in Cymru. And the 'A', what's more, that was going to send me off to the Eisteddfod (where I had a piece of prose in the open competition for learners) in a mood of cheerful enthusiasm.

To repeat myself boringly, I don't think there's an end to the process of learning Welsh. Once you make the changeover to living noticeable chunks of your life through the medium of the language, your speech will continue to become richer, more colloquial and more varied for the rest of your life. However, since this is a book about learning Welsh, and since neither you nor I want it to go on forever, I have to choose a place to stop, and the most appropriate place of all would have to be Tyddewi. Two years exactly since I started my journey home towards the language, and my third National Eisteddfod was a marking post for how far I had come. For the first time, I was going to be at the Eisteddfod for more than just a day, and for the first time I was going to be a real part of this huge multi-coloured made-up thing that is so close to the truth of being Welsh. I'd come far enough to be at the Eisteddfod as more than someone simply looking through a shop window and wanting every single sweet on offer – I'd come far enough to be nearly home.

Some Sex and a Hill

Some Sex and a Hill

Pennod 17 – Tuag Adref

I'd taken two days off work, and was driving all the way down to deepest, darkest De Gorllewin Cymru on the Wednesday evening, with the seats down and a mattress fixed neatly into the back of my car. I'd learnt about Eisteddfodau and rain by now, and I was taking no risks. None of this camping malarkey for me – I'm far more suited to the luxury of a five star hotel, or, failing that, a mattress in the back of my car. Doesn't sound all that luxurious to you? It would, if you'd just been woken in the middle of a] the night and b] a wild thunderstorm because c] your tent had been blown away. When it became clear that despite everything that people said smugly about how lovely the beginning of the week had been, the second half of Eisteddfod Genedlaethol Tyddewi was in fact going to be an uncontrolled mudfest, my mattress/car combo began to look like a stroke of sheer genius. What's more, it meant that the slightly schizophrenic nature of the Eisteddfod, which was in many ways the Solfach Eisteddfod, home to Meic Stevens, wasn't a problem. I just drove wherever I wanted, and slept wherever I'd parked the car, which turned out mostly to be in the car park of the Harbour Inn.

This time, instead of sidling into the Cymuned tent on a strictly low profile 'sign up and get the hell out without making any grammatical mistakes' kind of mission, I was helping man it, and it had doubled in size. What's more, we didn't have the Tories next door any more – no, we'd graduated to Cymdeithas yr Iaith, which made for some interesting balances of tension during the week.

Now I know what it's like to spend more than a day at the Eisteddfod, I can't imagine ever going back to just popping in for a day trip visit. The apparently endless round of concerts and sessions in the pub and protests and sweets and encouraging people to join up and choirs and readings and recitations and more sessions in the pub and if you're me more sweets and on and on and on… it's a heady mix, intoxicating in every possible meaning of the word. I was meeting new, interesting people every day, mostly in the Harbour Inn in Solfach, and being surrounded by a sort of permanent, non-stop conversation in Welsh, with all sorts of delightfully drunken people claiming they would never have realised I was a learner if I hadn't told them. Clearly, enough alcohol not only makes learners *feel* as though they speak Welsh better, it also gives first-language speakers the aural equivalent of beer goggles – a perfect combination! Even when I found myself talking to people like Ioan from Crymych, who has the strongest south Walian accent that I've ever heard, it all seemed easy and natural. My sense that I had fallen through into a world that I'd only ever previously been able to watch on television was heightened even further by the stray cast members of Pobol y Cwm that you'd find yourself elbowing past on your way to the bar. An occasional drunken urge would come over me to thank them tearfully for the invaluable practice they and their subtitles had given me over the last couple of years, but fortunately some sort of reverse echo of the embarrassment that would have made me feel once I'd sobered up always kept me from giving in.

And the world seemed suddenly full of beautiful girls talking Welsh, which reminded me that having got to the point where a fair amount of my work was done through the medium of Welsh, and where 99% of my socialising was done through the medium of Welsh, there was just one last piece of that old jigsaw missing. It was time for me to find a lovely first-language girl who was tolerant enough of learners to put up with going out with me, and helping me achieve my goal of Welsh 24/7 (sleep permitting, but there's a good chance that if I talk in my sleep these days, it's probably in Welsh). No, I'm sorry, this isn't where it's going to get steamy, because this particular part of my drive to learn Welsh remains a work in progress. It's tricky enough being essentially quite a shy person (yes I am), but being shy in a second language just compounds the difficulties.

I'm typing this quite slowly now, with a certain sense of wistful reluctance, because there's just one last piece of the Eisteddfod that I want to tell you about, and then it will be time for me to stop writing in English. After three novels, one children's book and a travelogue about driving across America (no, none of which have been published, so maybe it's about time for me to give up anyway), as well as several poems a month for most of my adult life (some of which have in fact cropped up in quite respectable poetry magazines, to my surprise), it's time to type my last few words in English.

Why?

Because of what I've said several times before – using English damages your Welsh. If I'm to have any chance at all of writing in Welsh, and I would dearly love to, I need to stop writing in English. I've noticed this particularly in the last couple of weeks – writing a few thousand words a day in English has really had a knock-on effect on my spoken Welsh, because of course I have to think in English in order to be able to write the stuff. I'm already looking forward to getting back to being almost entirely Welsh in thought and speech for almost all the time, but I have to admit that the prospect of not writing in English any more… well, it's a little intimidating. You see, I've always been quite passionate about language, and English has been my language for over thirty years, so I have a great deal of love for it. I just happen to love Welsh more. That's why it's important that I take this step – because it means I'm committing to Welsh. Either I write in Welsh, or I don't write again. Writing has always been a large part of what defines me, so if that isn't enough of a kick up the backside to get my written Welsh to where it needs to be, nothing could be.

And I came *third* in the prose competition for learners, by the way, which means that I have got to get better. I really meant it about being psychotically competitive.

Okay, here's the last thing I wanted to tell you about. Of course I'd intended to go to all the rallies available in the Eisteddfod anyway, whatever nonsense Rhodri Morgan spouted about how it wasn't appropriate to campaign for the future of the language in the middle of its greatest celebration, but I hadn't actually intended to get involved to the point of cross-dressing.

Perhaps I'd better explain.

If I'd been thinking a bit more quickly, I would have noticed that the Cymuned tent was getting suspiciously empty as Dewi bedecked himself in skirts and shawls and headscarves to be Rebecca, ready to smash a symbolic gate in front of Pabell Llywodraeth y Cynulliad. There were only two of us left by the time he looked around, and roared that he couldn't exactly re-enact Merched Beca without some bloody daughters, and then suddenly there were enough people to help me get dressed, and check that my skirts and shawls matched, and that my bum didn't look too big, and I floated through it all with a feeling of puzzled detachment, wondering when exactly it was that I had agreed to quite such a public gender swap.

By the time we'd carried the gate to the back of the crowd, I really was getting an uncharacteristic feeling that I ought to brush my hair, even though I've got a crew cut, and colour-coding in general was right at the front of my mind until we'd womanhandled the gate to the front of the crowd, and I realised that Dewi was going to be smashing it with a bloody gigantic hammer. What's more, as he prepared for action, looking like a Viking god of thunder after a particularly riotous stag night, it seemed clear that he was aiming directly at my hand, and I suddenly wanted to see some evidence of his qualifications for gate-smashing. I mean, 'I'd give my right hand for it' is meant to be a figure of speech, not an invitation to violence. Talk about putting my principles to the test.

It has a happy ending, you'll be pleased to hear. As all the best stories do, and as the fight for the future of the Welsh language will, too – because love is what defines us, and anything defended for the sake of love cannot be destroyed. Don't you watch enough films? Dewi, it turned out, had obviously been practising smashing gates ever since he was a babe in arms, and I still have both my hands. Of course, I *would* give my right hand for Cymru Rydd, but preferably not until after I've finished with it, if that's okay. And by the time we'd sneaked off to the back of the crowd, leaving the shattered remains of the fence where it was, I was almost reluctant to get rid of my headscarf and shawl. I'd never realised how much *warmer* women's clothes are.

So, here we are. That's how I came home, the story of healing a wrong done to my parents and grandparents and to me myself before I was born. Remember Matthew Arnold? 'Sooner or later, the difference of language between Wales and England will probably be effaced… an event which is socially and politically so desirable.' Well, we're going to prove you wrong, Mr Arnold.

Oh, and I seem to recall promising you that I'd prove that sex is much better in Welsh. I will, too – in the last chapter. Yes, there's just one more to go. One slight catch – you'll need to learn Welsh before you bother turning the page. And of course, if you do, you won't need me to prove it to you – because you'll have experienced it for yourself. Go on. You know it makes sense.

[Oh, one last thing – if you appear, however briefly, in these pages, and we haven't been in touch for a while, I'd *love* to hear from you. The best way to get hold of me is probably on Twitter, where I'm @aranjones – where you're also welcome to come and shout at me in general terms, if you need to kill a little time.]

[Oh, and one more last thing – since learning Welsh, my life has become increasingly unpredictable. I wrote my own Welsh course and co-founded SaySomethinginWelsh.com with the wonderful Iestyn ap Dafydd – the 25 half-hour sessions of Level 1 are free, if you're trying to learn at the moment.

I'll get around to telling that story one day, too – it's provisionally titled '*A Lunatic's Guide To Building a Language Course*' – if you'd like to hear when it's available, follow me on Twitter @aranjones or sign up to the SaySomethinginWelsh weekly email (go here https://www.saysomethingin.com/welsh/info/faq and scroll down to 'How can I get access to the SSiW weekly email?').]

Some Sex and a Hill

Some Sex and a Hill

Pennod 18 – 'Diolch, o ddiolch i bawb.'

A dyna ni – mae hynny'n well, 'tydy?

Gobeithio, gyda llaw, bod chi ddim yn disgwyl
Cymraeg *graenus* yn fan hyn – cam cyntaf ar y daith
ydy o, wedi'r cyfan. Ac wrth gwrs fydd 'na ddim
ffasiwn beth â sôn am ambell cwtsh dwi efallai wedi
cael trwy gyfrwng y Gymraeg, am na fysai hynny ddim
yn barchus, na fysai? Ac mae Mam yn deall myw o'r
iaith nag y mae hi'n cyfaddef bob tro, a dydw i *ddim*
eisiau peltan, diolch yn fawr.

Y cwbl dw i eisiau gwneud yn fan hyn, dweud y gwir,
ydy diolch i'r bobl rhoddodd gymorth a chefnogaeth i
fi yn ystod fy nhaith tuag at yr iaith, boed fel
athro/athrawes neu fel ffrindiau mewn tafarndai.
Rheiny sydd wedi'i gwneud hi'n bosibl i mi adennill fy
etifeddiaeth golledig, ac adennill bywyd llawn
Cymreig. Dw i'n ddiolchgar dros ben i bob un
ohonynt, ond yn enwedig i Haf a Jo (ac wrth gwrs i
Felicity, Swyn, Cêt, Lleucu, Twm ac Elin!), i Non, i

Anwen, i Seimon, i Mared, i fwy nag un Richard, i
Gwen a Delyth a Mair, i Iwan, i Rhys, i Non a Nige, i
Siwan, i Rob, i David ac i'r hen goes o Lydaw, Brieg,
sydd wedi cael ei dynnu allan i ddwyn perswâd ar
fewnfudwyr i ddysgu Cymraeg mwy nag unwaith,
chwarae teg iddo.

Ac i Catrin, wrth gwrs, er bod hynny'n stori
gwahanol! Mae wedi bod yn fraint dod i'w nabod
nhw, a dw i'n teimlo hynny i'r carn – yn yr un ffordd
â dw i'n teimlo'r fraint bob tro dwi'n naill ai'n dweud
neu'n clywed rhywbeth yn y Gymraeg.

Clywais i unwaith rywun ar y radio yn dweud bod
Plaid Cymru yn mynd i symud i ffordd oddi wrth yr
hen ramant wirion o gyfeirio at y Gymraeg fel 'iaith y
nefoedd' – gobeithio ddim, oherwydd byddai hynny'n
symud i ffordd oddi wrth fy mhleidlais i hefyd, gan
fod y Gymraeg *yn* iaith y nefoedd i fi, ac felly y bydd
hi am byth.

Manufactured by Amazon.ca
Bolton, ON

20427601R00136